JUST A GIRL FROM DETROIT

Just A Girl From Detroit

SHAY COLE,
RENATO L. FRIDAY, NAYA
PERRY-EDDINGS, TIFFANY
BARBER, & SHANNON
CAIN-WOMACK

Creative Chameleon

Contents

Dedication   vi

One	MEET TIFFANY BARBER	1
Two	MEET RENATO L. FRIDAY	4
Three	MEET NAYA PERRY-EDDINGS	34
Four	MEET SHANNON CAIN-WOMACK	42
Five	MEET SHAY COLE	78

About The Authors   110

Dedications

Tiffany "T.Barb" Barber
Dedicated to all the Retired Hoodrats

Shannon Cain-Womack - Model
I want to Thank God for giving me the strength to keep on keeping on! I dedicate this book to my family, the ones that are still with me and the ones with our Heavenly Father. I love you all! I also dedicate this book to my friends. I love you all. And lastly, I dedicate this book to all of the children who are not able to share their stories. And to all of the attempted kidnapping survivors. You are not alone. One love. "No Weapon That Is Formed Against Thee Shall Prosper" Isaiah 54:17

Naya "DJ Royalty" Perry-Eddings
I dedicate this book to everyone who showed me love and support in any kind of way throughout my life. ESPECIALLY to the ones who told me "I cant" because in elementary school Mrs. Clark

told me personally "CAN'T is NOT in YOUR vocabulary!"

Author Renato L. Friday

I dedicate this to my babies, my divas-in-training. No matter what happens in life or what anybody tells you, NEVER give up. Continue to pursue your dreams and appreciate the journey, good and bad. God gave you so many talents, so make sure you use them to the best of your ability. You girls are my inspiration, motivation, and reasons to keep going, and I'm happy to have you all on this journey called life. I love you girls to infinity and beyond.

Shay Cole - Philanthropist & Entrepreneur

I dedicate this book to to everyone with a vision. Write the vision and make it plain.

Copyright © 2024 Creative Chameleon.

All rights reserved. No part of this publication may be reproduced, distributed, or transmitted in any form or by any means, including photocopying, recording, or other electronic or mechanical methods, without the prior written permission of the publisher, except in the case of brief quotations embodied in critical reviews and certain other noncommercial uses permitted by copyright law. For permission requests, email the publisher, addressed "Attention: Permissions Coordinator," at the email address below.

ISBN: 978-1-7378961-9-7 (Paperback)
ISBN: 978-1-7378961-8-0 (Ebook)

First printing edition 2024.

Creative Chameleon
contactme@shaycole.com

Chapter One

MEET TIFFANY BARBER

There are certain qualities Detroit women possess that announce our presence before we enter a room and I am Detroit from head to toe. There's a hypnotic mixture of perseverance, grit and perfume that make us special like no other. We are born winners.

My parents met fresh out of prison in a halfway house and could not stand each other. It is hilarious that although they hated each other my parents shared the responsibility of raising me. I wish more parents would do a better job of that. They understood the importance of a child having two parents so they duked it out all while being present and active. My mother was a hardcore gangster with a dash of mental illness and a liking for zoos zoos and wams

wams, while my father, who also liked wams wams, was extremely successful until he lost his kidneys. I grew up hustling hard and acting like an adult. My circumstances required that I grow up fast. I was very "grown" but I loved school which allowed me to escape hood life. My education led me to a HBCU and the rest is history. I am an official Retired Hoodrat.

I have persevered through many major life changes but one of the most significant was leaving Detroit to go to college in New Orleans. I had never been to the south and went alone. I remember all of the parents staring and waiting for an adult to come stand in line with me. I was afraid I would get to the front of the line and they wouldn't have my name, but thank God I was on the housing list. That day will always be ingrained in my mind as the first time I put myself first. It was difficult to stay the course and complete my Bachelor's Degree, but the "Detroit" in me would not allow me to quit. After leaving college I went into the social work field and worked for the State of Michigan. The career life was so different but coming from a hoodrat lifestyle to working for the state was the ultimate come, yet something was still missing. It wasn't until I was introduced to my passion did I understand the void I felt despite overcoming so much adversity...I discovered comedy and decided to go after my dreams. In addition to being a social worker I was an entrepreneur so I devised a plan and stepped out on faith. I still have a hard time believing

I haven't worked an orthodox job in over 5 years…Life is all about the pivot.

Life is a continuous lesson. It's not about what happens to you but how you handle it. Take heed to every sign, make yourself a priority because no one cares about your excuses, only your results.

Chapter Two

MEET RENATO L. FRIDAY

Whaddup doe! My name is Renato and I was born and raised in the beautiful city of Detroit. My life started on the streets of Archdale and Plymouth, and it migrated over to Oakman and Joy Rd. I am an only child who has been in both private and public schools. I have 4 beautiful daughters who drive me crazy everyday, but I wouldn't change them for the world. I love music, poetry, reading, and writing.

In 2021, I officially became an author by publishing my first book, which was a children's book. After that, I went on to publish my memoir. I have gone through my fair share of ups and downs, and decided to share my story after a tumultuous situation occurred between me and my mother. I also published a poetry book that same year and have since written a novel and several novellas. I have been an author now for three years and I'm so glad I decided to embark on this journey. It has been the most therapeutic and invigorating accomplishment thus far. I love to write and I've always been a reader since childhood. So with that being said, let's dig a little into my backstory.

I was born an only child and raised in a two family household. Both my parents had very good jobs working at Michcon, now known as DTE. I was lucky to have a close relationship with both my parents, having a unique bond between the two. I always wanted a sibling, preferably a sister, but unfortunately, that didn't happen. Being an only child got lonely, but I did have a lot of friends from the neighborhood and school. Like most parents, they wanted me to have the best education, so my school life started at Children's Learning Institute, a private school located off Six Mile and Southfield Freeway. We had to wear these ugly blue plaid uniforms.

That's also where I took dance classes and loved doing recitals. I also learned how to type at the age of six, which has contributed to my typing skills to this day. I was an honor student, straight A's and B's. I stayed at Children's Learning Center until it was time for second grade. Then my parents decided to put me in St. Scholastica, a private catholic school around the corner from my granny. I stayed there and graduated from eighth grade... barely. My grades were impeccable up until sixth grade then my grades started to drop. I'm not sure what contributed to it, but the last three years of St. Scholastica were a struggle. I graduated off a wing and a prayer.

Mackenzie High School was my school of choice for the next four years. Neither of my parents wanted me to go there, even though it was my dad's alma mater. They didn't want me to go because it was so close to our house. I literally walked 2-3 blocks to get there. My original choice was Benedictine High School, but my mom refused to keep paying for me to go to a private catholic school, so Mackenzie was my only other choice. My parents didn't have to re-arrange their schedules to accommodate taking me to and from school. Going here was the best decision because I really loved it. I was a little nervous at first because I didn't know anyone. I didn't go to any of the neighborhood schools like everyone else, so I was the odd ball out.

Outside of the fact that we got to wear whatever we wanted to school, it was just like any other school. Private schools are known for being a little strict and more organized, which they should be since our parents were paying for our education, but the same crap happens in private schools that happen in public schools: fights, gossip, cliques, inappropriate language or behavior, standard teenage stuff. My grades even went back up which put me back on the honor roll. I wasn't miss popular, but I did make a decent amount of friends. I mostly hung with the boys on the football team. Those were my brothers. I consider myself one of those people that gets along with anybody, so if I had beef with anybody, it wasn't on account of me. I was overly friendly and goofy as hell, but I think that's what made me get along with everyone because I was just being me and not trying to fit in with a certain group of kids. If I was asked what part of school I liked, I'd absolutely say high school, but had I gone to college, I'd probably say that because I've heard stories of how fun college life is. I tried community college right after high school, but I wasn't focused nor ready to go. I only went because my mom made me. That was a big mistake because I failed my first semester and never went back.

The end of my freshman year was one of the hardest years of my life. My dad passed away from meningococcal meningitis at the age of 43. I was 14 years old. He was sick for two weeks prior to his passing, and it's still a shock to me after 26 years. For a man that was one of the healthiest people I'd ever known to just suddenly become ill with no warning was crazy. My dad took every vitamin you could think of and ran 26 miles a day; before and after work. He was a health nut because when he was younger, say in his 20s, he didn't like the way he looked. He considered himself to be overweight because his belly stuck out a little further than he wanted, so he made the necessary lifestyle changes to become a healthier and happier him. He played several sports: basketball, baseball, bowling, and also ran the Detroit Free Press marathons as well as the Boston Marathons. My daddy was very active in his church and had just come back from a men's retreat in the Smokey Mountains with some fellow church members when he got sick. He took a day off work, something he never did, claiming he didn't feel good. My mom went to work and I went to school. My mom called to check on my dad and he was still in bed, which was very unlike him.

When she got home, she checked his temperature and it was 105 degrees. He'd also had an accident and was very delirious due to the fever. We immediately rushed him to urgent care where they didn't want to see him due to his extremely high temp. We ended up taking him to the closest Henry Ford clinic where they took him in the back to run tests. They informed us that he had jaundice and was being transferred to Henry Ford hospital to run more tests and he'd be staying overnight. When we got there, they told us that he was in a coma and that they didn't think he was going to make it through the night. My stomach was in knots and I broke down crying once I got home and called my best friend. To think that I could lose my dad so soon just knocked the wind out of me. Even though I was close to both my parents equally, I was a daddy's girl. The next day, we went to see him and he was still in a coma. Seeing my daddy hooked up to machines, tubes down his throat, was unforgettable for a 14 year old girl; and after several tests were ran, that's when they diagnosed him with meningococcal meningitis.

It was a rare form, so the treatment options were slim to none. There was no cure. We visited him everyday and my mom even brought his walkman with gospel music and sermons, anything to try and lift his spirits and get him to wake up. After a week went by, he finally woke up. He was still connected to the machines. Once unhooked, he was barely able to talk, so I tried to give him a cup of water. He didn't want me to serve it to him and it hurt my feelings. My dad's extended family/friends were there with us when he woke, so I decided to go into the waiting room to gather myself. They came to console me before I went back to see him, and that's when the doctors hit us with some more disturbing news. After examining my dad's legs, they saw that he wasn't getting circulation to them. They were covered in huge blisters. They gave us two options to help him: amputate both his legs or insert catheters to help with blood flow, but with the second option, he would be at risk of bleeding somewhere else in his body. My dad being the athlete that he was, automatically denied the amputation.

After he made his decision, that was the last time we saw him awoke. The procedure caused my dad to hemorrhage in his brain. While doing surgery to stop the bleeding, he suffered several strokes and ended up in a vegetative state. My mom had to make the most devastating decision: keep him alive in the condition he was in, or allow him to die peacefully knowing that he would never want to live the rest of his life like that. My father took his last breath on June 5, 1997, 33 days after his 43rd birthday. My mom got the phone call right before it was time for me to get ready for school. Yes, I still went to school that day. When she told me he passed, I didn't even cry. I just continued to go about my morning. I think I had cried all my tears during the two weeks he was still alive and knowing what was going to happen didn't alarm me. They had already told us the outcome, so there was nothing to be surprised about.

When I arrived at school, my classmates asked how he was doing, and I informed them of what happened. Everybody asked me why I was there, and I'm like what am I supposed to do? Stay at home and watch my mom call everybody, then make funeral arrangements? I didn't want to do that. My mom hadn't cried not once that I knew of, but everyone handles sickness and grief differently, so I didn't judge her. By the time I got to 6th hour, which was my history class, my teacher told me to go home and be with my mom. I only had one class left after that so I left. I called my best friend and told her what happened. That's all I remember until the day of the funeral. My dad's funeral was on June 13, 1997, two days before Father's Day and eleven days before my 15th birthday. Forty-three was still very young. My mom broke down crying walking down the aisle approaching the casket. She froze halfway there and I had to help guide her. Since it was family hour, we were the first to see my daddy before everyone else arrived. Since they had to perform brain surgery, we had found him a nice African hat to match his suit to cover up the part that was shaved. He'd worn an afro my entire life and never cut it low because he always said he felt he had an odd-shaped head, so that was his signature look. I never thought I would see my daddy like that. Laying in a casket. Never being able to hear him call me "Susie" again. I don't remember when or why he started calling me that, but it was something that only he did and made our bond unique.

The year I got pregnant with my oldest child, I was 24. I'd been with my then boyfriend for three years before we conceived this blessing. I was nervous to tell my mom even though I was grown and living on my own, but it was the fact that I was pregnant without being married. Our family was overly religious and I was raised to get married first then have kids. Well, that had always been my plan and me and my boyfriend had entertained the thought and started calling each other wifey and hubby. I had been feeling tired and nauseated for weeks and one of my coworkers actually asked me if I was pregnant and I told her I didn't think so. She had three kids so she would know, but I was still in denial of the thought. I was very close with my mom, so I would call her all the time from work, especially when something juicy was going on. This particular day, there was an unexpected murder at my job. I worked at a hotel in Southfield and a guy strangled his girlfriend to death because he found out she had been sleeping around with his brother. The cops called me to warn me they were coming up there and when they did, it was a swarm of them. Sadly, one of my housekeepers was the one who found her unconscious in the bed face down.

While I told her all the drama that was unfolding, I also informed her that I had been feeling nauseous and tired and the first thing she asked me was if I was pregnant and like I told my coworker, I didn't think so. She then proceeded to ask if we were using protection and I told her no, plus my periods had been irregular since I started at age 14 so there really was no way of knowing without taking a test. I went to the pharmacy after work, bought a test, took it once I got home, and it came back positive. The shock on my face was a mixture of nervousness and joy. I was going to have my first baby, but how was my boyfriend going to feel? I called him as soon as I finished calming down and told him. He didn't believe me at first because he felt after being together 3 years and no surprises happening that maybe it was impossible but nope, there was a bun in the oven. He told me to send him a picture of the test which I did and his next reaction was 'WOW'. He said he would see me when he got home (we were living together around this time) and I called my mom next to tell her the news. She wasn't surprised but happy. I asked for her gynecologist's number so I could call her the next day for an appointment. I'd been to her before and loved her personality. I called my best friend and told her the news too. She was happy as well. My mom went with me to my doctor's appointment.

After I went in the back, they had me take a

pregnancy test and it confirmed that I was indeed pregnant, 8 weeks and 2 days to be exact. My doctor used a doppler to hear my baby's heartbeat and did an ultrasound. To hear my baby's heartbeat and see the little peanut shaped figure on the screen was surreal. I was so happy for those first moments, I even got to take my ultrasound pictures home. I called and confirmed the information with both my boyfriend and my best friend. When I got home, I showed my boyfriend the ultrasound. He was still in shock but happy. He instantly told his parents and they were just as ecstatic. My baby's due date was 10/3/2007. We found out I was having a girl in May and everybody was happy, especially the grandmothers. My boyfriend's mom had 3 boys, no girls and wanted a daughter so bad. Now she was going to have a granddaughter, plus this would be the first grandchild for her and my mom. My pregnancy was a breeze to me, no complications, and I was all belly, looking like I swallowed a watermelon. Everything was going great until one day I was at work and the man that had robbed us once, attempted the second time but I had the door locked, came back a third time and barely covered his face.

I was now almost 7 months pregnant. It was broadlight and he had a gun pointed in my face. He forced me to go to the back office with the gun now pointed in my back. It was one of the scariest moments of my life because this man could literally take me and my unborn baby's life. Thank God he didn't harm us. I watched his every move on the cameras. He got what he wanted and left quickly. I called my manager as soon as the coast was clear. I locked myself in the office until the police came. My job was so inconsiderate that they didn't offer to find someone to finish my shift nor finish it themselves. They just suggested that I do like we'd been doing and keep the doors locked. If anything would've happened to me or my baby, they would've had a full blown lawsuit on their hands. Due to the evidence from watching the cameras, a few of my coworkers were able to identify the man, who turned out to be an ex-employee who'd been fired some time before I started. We all went to court to testify but I was lied to by the prosecutor because they told me that we all had to take the stand when in actuality, it was only me that had to look at the man that could've taken me and my baby's life. I was nervous because I'd never been in a courtroom, let alone on the witness stand. And what do you know, his girlfriend was there also and she looked to be around 5 months pregnant. How ironic.

After the trial was over, I went on maternity leave. I started having contractions on October 1st. My boyfriend took me to the hospital and I was only 1cm dilated. They called my doctor and informed her what was going on. She suggested that I walk around for an hour to see if I would progress before making the decision of keeping me or sending me home. After an hour of walking around the hospital floor, I dilated to 3cm and my doctor allowed me to stay. I got a private room and the pains were getting stronger. I didn't want an epidural because I'd heard horror stories, but the pain was getting worse to the point that I started crying. My mom, my boyfriend's mom, and the nurse tried to convince me to get something and didn't want me to suffer. The nurse suggested Demerol which would be injected intravenously, but the down side was it would make me high but not alleviate the pain. I didn't want to feel NOTHING, so I broke down and got the epidural which was the best decision I could've made. The procedure wasn't bad and I was able to get some much needed sleep. When I woke up, it's like the epidural never happened. The pain shot through me and I clinched the side rails every time a contraction hit. After 19 hours and 43 minutes, my baby girl finally arrived. She was 7lbs, 6oz. I was tired and happy. They asked if I was going to breastfeed, which I planned on doing, but I was too exhausted, so I opted for the bottle. I never did breastfeed her, even after that.

The day we came home from the hospital it was hot as hell, like 80 degrees in OCTOBER. I had packed our bags with fall clothes. Even when we took her to her first doctor's appointment a couple days after we were discharged, it was still extremely hot. I had my baby in a long sleeve onesie and a blanket covering her face in her carseat, so when we uncovered her, she was sweating. I felt so bad that I was overheating my baby, but I wanted to make sure she didn't get sick. Her immune system was in a compromising position due to her being a newborn. I stayed with my mom for 3 months while on maternity leave so she could help me with the baby. She was a good baby too, sleeping throughout the night. We didn't have a lot of visitors because I didn't allow it. I didn't want all those outside germs contaminating my baby. After my maternity leave was over, I had to go back to work, and my mom watched my daughter. I would call and check on her throughout my shift and like I said, she was a good baby.

When I got pregnant with my second daughter, to say my mom wasn't happy would be an understatement. She was livid! Very disappointed in me. She couldn't understand after all the bullshit I went through with my boyfriend why I would go and get pregnant again. I was already practically taking care of my first born alone and after the fiasco of him putting his hands on me and throwing my car keys in the alley, leaving me and my best friend stranded in the dark, in the cold, and in the hood, I should've never let him touch me again. She was right! I should've ended it after that situation happened. The level of disrespect given by him, embarrassing me in front of my best friend, his friend, and cousin was irreversible. I agree that my mom was right, but it was too late and I don't believe in abortion. My boyfriend wasn't too happy and made the statement that he either wasn't ready for another kid or how was he going to take care of another kid. Like I said, I don't believe in abortion, so we'd both have to deal with it.

I got pregnant around Valentine's Day 2010. When I found out, I was 10 weeks. I was on a different insurance, so I had a different doctor. A male one this time; something I never wanted. Not going against male doctors, but I feel more comfortable with women due to the fact they know our bodies better and the majority of them have kids which means they can better understand what we go through and can empathize with me. My first interaction with him was unpleasant. His bedside manner, as my mother calls it, was rude in my opinion. He tried to tell me about my body and when I conceived, which I knew exactly when that happened, and assumed my due date to be sooner than it should've been. He had my due date set sometime in late October which means I would've conceived in January like my first. I knew 100% that was wrong, but he was insistent on that being it.

I was so dissatisfied with his mannerism that I was looking into other doctors. For whatever reason, I decided to give him another chance and go to him for my follow-up appointment. His demeanor was a bit lighter and after spending more time with him, I realized that that was his personality and he wasn't being rude on purpose. He set me up for an ultrasound at Sinai hospital and we found out we were having another girl. We told both our mothers again and just like last time, they were happy. Another girl to add to the family. When they took measurements of my baby it was alarming to my doctor that she was not developing the way she should for her gestational period, so he ordered another ultrasound. Apparently the bridge of her nose was a sign of Down's Syndrome.

That was a shocker to all of us and the doctor at the hospital hinted at abortion due to this possible diagnosis and told me I had 2 weeks to make a decision as I was almost 24 weeks and abortions were not allowed after that.

Another ultrasound was done a week later and the ultrasound technician is the one that figured out that my original due date and measurements were wrong. I wasn't as far along as my doctor had assumed and my baby was developing correctly and right on time. I told the technician that my doctor didn't want to believe that I knew when I conceived and went off whatever birth chart they use. I knew he was wrong and he apologized once I went in for another checkup. My "new" due date was now November 11th. I went into the hospital on the evening of November 2nd. While I was in labor, my baby's heart rate was dropping. I couldn't see the monitors but my boyfriend and his mother could. She gasped and nobody let me know what was going on. All my doctor told me was that I needed to get on all fours. The umbilical cord was wrapped around her neck and they needed to unravel as much as they could because she was losing oxygen.

Once I flipped back over, they immediately told me to push. I pushed as hard as I could a few times until she was finally delivered. They whisked her away to the table and finished removing the umbilical cord that was still wrapped around her neck. I heard the precious sound of my new baby crying and I asked if she was okay. Her dad responded, "yeah. She just pooped on the nurse." I burst out laughing while in tears. After they finally cleaned her up, I was able to hold my beautiful 6lb 13 oz baby in my arms. She was perfect and so tiny to me but I'm glad she was healthy. After all the ups and downs I had endured over the course of 8 years, I finally broke things off with my boyfriend. There was no fixing us and once the girls came into the picture it just made things worse. I refused to take care of 2 kids and a grown man that wasn't trying hard enough to make things right. I wasn't going to waste another 8 years hoping that things would change and get better. I had to do what was best for me and my daughters. I had already moved back in with my mom after losing my apartment and everything inside so what was there to hold onto? My daughters and I deserved better, with or without their dad.

I remained single for a year after I left my kids' father. I wasn't interested in anyone and just needed to focus on the girls who were now 6 and 3. I had a new job making a little more money, so hopefully I could be back on my feet again. I started seeing someone not too long after but things didn't work out, which was fine because it seemed there was someone else who had their eyes on me. He asked me if I had a sweetie for Sweetest Day, which I replied no. Next thing I know, he came back with 2 small bottles of Moet, some chocolate covered almonds, and a champagne flute. I was flattered. I thanked him for the gift and we started dating after that. We dated for 2 months before making it official and having sex, and not too long after that, I got pregnant with my third child. This would be his first child. He was a divorcee and out of the 8 years he was married, never conceived a child. He thought he couldn't have kids... until he met me, little miss fertile.

I was amazed at how quickly I got pregnant, and it goes to show you that condoms aren't always effective because the one we used broke. I also don't know how long he had that condom either so that could've contributed too. I wasn't going to introduce him to my girls until I was sure this was turning into something serious and long term but since I was with child, I had no choice but to let them meet and see how they got along. Lucky for him, they liked him. The beginning of this pregnancy was not the best. A domino effect of events began happening that were unexpected and almost ended my new relationship. My mother and I had got into a huge argument that turned into a fight and caused me to go to the emergency room. My mom had bit me on my arm because she thought I was going to hit her which I wasn't. No matter how angry I am at her, I would never hit her. I was trying to keep her from calling the police on me and kicking me and the girls out.

When I arrived at the emergency room and told them what happened, they looked at me weird. They were trying to figure out how someone, your own mother at that, would bite you and to the extent of revealing flesh and having to make me get a tetanus shot. And I was 12 weeks pregnant with my third daughter. I was still in shock too. My own mother caused me bodily harm trying to protect herself from me and all I was trying to do was protect myself and my girls. I had to call off work that day and checked into a hotel for the week. I couldn't go back there and honestly didn't want to because I didn't feel safe. The night I checked in, I went to the Meijer down the street and bought as much clothes and food as I could that didn't have to be cooked. Our room had a fridge and microwave, but no stove. Thank God I had just got my taxes back because me and the girls would literally be homeless had I not. I spent the first night crying myself to sleep. My boyfriend stayed the night and held me as I cried. All I could ask was why. Why did this happen? Why would she do this? I did stop by her house to get some more clothes, the girls' uniforms, but nothing more. When I got there, I couldn't get in the house.

My key worked, but she had a security device on the back of the door to keep possible thieves out, hell, maybe even me, because it was ironic how she put that on the door AFTER we had our altercation and I left. In the midst of all this, gossiping women at work were trying to cause problems for me and my boyfriend. They were saying that my boyfriend couldn't be the father of my unborn baby because I was messing with someone else before we got together. What those nosey heffas didn't know was that me and that guy had already stopped kicking it before I dated and slept with my boyfriend. Plus, you can't be pregnant for a whole year. He was so ignorant that he listened to them, and apparently his parents who felt some kind of way. His parents told them that they knew someone who it happened to, but that had nothing to do with me. I wasn't the type of woman who went around sleeping with every Tom, Dick, and Harry and didn't know who her baby daddy was.

They didn't know anything about me and with that being said, he had the audacity to ask for a DNA test. I was taken aback but never said no. I knew who I slept with. The females at work were just jealous because my boyfriend spoiled me with attention and love, something they were obviously lacking if they were so worried about us. Me and the girls stayed in the hotel until my money ran out, which was about 2-3 months. It was so hard being there; having to eat out every day and having to find a babysitter most days because my mom didn't even want to watch her own grandkids. But we survived and begrudgingly had to go back to my mom's house because we had nowhere to go and no apartments were within reason. She allowed us to come back and I tried to keep the peace as much as I could under her roof. I left the hotel I met my boyfriend at for a better opportunity at another hotel. It was an hour away, but it was more money and a desk job. And they hired me while I was 8 ½, 9 months pregnant, which was a blessing.

One of the sales ladies that worked at my old hotel and came to the new one had referred me for the job.

They hired me on the spot. The people at my old job wondered where I'd gone and if I really got a new job in my condition and my boyfriend told them I did, but he didn't divulge any other information. It was none of their nosey ass business. I got the training I needed, then went on maternity leave. I had gone to visit my new job the day I got induced to pick up my paycheck. I was a week overdue, so I was going into the hospital that night. I was so ready for this girl to come out. My oldest birthday was the following day and I wanted to be home to celebrate her special day. This baby was almost born on her sister's birthday but I was like nope, let's get this over with. After 10 hours, my 3rd baby girl was finally born weighing 6lb, 7oz. She was my smallest baby. They allowed me to go home the next day, so we stopped at the grocery store so I could buy a birthday cake and surprise my baby girl. I was sore and going through the aftermath of giving birth, but I was determined to make her day just as special as the birth of her little sister. Her and her sister were so happy to see me, especially with a cake. We sang happy birthday, then it was back to baby duty.

It was not planned to get pregnant again, especially not so soon after having the last one, but I found myself with child. My baby wasn't even a year old yet. I guess I had a little too much fun during the 4th of July. Not too long after I found out I was pregnant and confirmed it with my doctor, I was fired from my job. My manager and I had a disagreement and I'm not the type of person to let someone like her mistreat me or my staff. Oh yeah, I had gotten a promotion by this time (by her), but I believe I was too intimidating for her. She was used to people being afraid of her until she met me. I was not backing down and if you were wrong, you were wrong. Period. But it was all good because I got another job within a month, even in my condition like before. My work ethics spoke volumes and I was a veteran in the hospitality game. I'm glad that my new manager took a chance on me just like my previous one. This pregnancy was so different, not in the sense that I had trouble, but because this was the only baby that was going to not be born in the fall.

I went through Halloween, Thanksgiving, Christmas, and New Year's pregnant. I was due in March and I couldn't wait. I had to go on maternity leave earlier than I expected because I was in alot of pain. The baby was pressing on my sciatic nerve, making it difficult to walk and stand sometimes. I had to get induced for the last time because this girl was just as stubborn as her sister and didn't want to come out, but at least I wasn't overdue, I just wasn't dilated past 1cm. People change like the weather and me being in labor proved that to be true for my boyfriend. Every pregnancy is different and you never know what to expect but to assume that you don't have to be there with your pregnant girlfriend through the entire process is insane. True, I was in labor with my 3rd baby for a while but that doesn't mean that you're allowed to leave me alone. He left me alone for 2 hours so that he could meet with his homeboy and smoke weed then feed his munchies. ANYTHING could've happened during that time, but that's just how inconsiderate I found him to be after being together for 3 years at this time.

Despite his behavior, he was back in time to see our daughter be born. She was 8lb, 9oz. She was my biggest baby and I almost thought she wasn't mine because my kids weight went down with each kid. No wonder I was in so much pain. She was a chunky baby. The day that I was released from the hospital, I had to drive myself home. This loser didn't have a car, so he drove mine from the hospital, then to the store to get some formula. I was breastfeeding this time since I knew this was my last baby but I didn't feel like she was getting enough milk from me, so I came up with a back up plan. After we left there, I dropped him off at home where I picked up her one year old sister, then we headed back to my mom's house. I had to carry an almost 9lb newborn, my hospital bag, and a diaper bag, all while sore and going through the aftermath of giving birth again.

My one year old was walking but I still had to assist her as well. With her, he asked to stay and help with her. With my baby, he didn't even attempt to offer to help. So I was left with a newborn, a toddler, and 2 older children while trying to breastfeed. My mom already did enough for me and the girls, so I tried not to bother her much, but this was strike two of how selfish and inconsiderate he was. Deciding to get my tubes tied was the best decision I could've ever made. I knew I didn't want to have anymore kids after what

I went through with my last 2 pregnancies, plus, I still wasn't married. Three months after giving birth, I had surgery to have my tubes removed per my doctor's choice to keep me from being at risk of ovarian cancer. That was my first time going under the knife, so I was on edge.

Luckily, they gave me something for my anxiety, then it was time for me to go to the operating room. The procedure was simple, three small incisions; two where my tubes would be located, and the other in my belly button. I saw my doctor right after they gave me anesthesia, and before I knew it, I was knocked out. I swear that was the best sleep ever. I woke up groggy and saw my boyfriend and kids sitting next to me. Once I got home, I was told to take it easy and get some rest, which is exactly what I did. I pretty much slept the rest of the day and my boyfriend stayed long enough to watch the kids while I did. When my baby was 6 months, I decided to quit my job. I was over my job and the graveyard shift, and decided to go back to school. I went to a trade school to be a pharmacy technician. My boyfriend was helping a little bit financially, but I eventually went back to working after a month.

I'm used to my own money and making my own money, so trying to depend on someone else was not happening. I got a part time job at another hotel downtown where one of my old coworkers referred me and one of my neighbors worked there too. Once February came around, I found a pharmacy to work at to get some hands-on experience; so I ended up working 2 part time jobs while going to school and taking care of four kids. Talk about supermom. The last straw of my boyfriend's selfishness was the day of my graduation. We weren't doing anything big but celebrating my accomplishments somehow was going to happen. This idiot didn't offer to take me and the kids out, nor did he stay to just spend time. He left. I don't know what he had to do and I didn't care at that point. Obviously it was more important than celebrating one of the biggest days of your now fiance's life. Oh yeah, I forgot to mention that we got engaged a month before I started school. Lucky me. I had quit the pharmacy once my externship had started and continued at the hotel until right before graduation. The place I externed at wanted to hire me but they wouldn't be able to match another job offer I had gotten. I was hired straight out of school to work at a closed door pharmacy, basically a warehouse. I didn't have to deal with any customers whatsoever. All I had to do was fill prescriptions and sometimes help pack and ship them out. I also had to take my certification to make more money, but I failed the first time. There are two kinds of certification tests, the hard one and the not so hard one. I passed the easier one with flying colors, so I was now a licensed and certified pharmacy technician.

    I was not expecting to bring in the year 2019 the way that I did. The day after New Year's, my mom decides to serve me with eviction papers, giving me

30 days to leave her home. We'd been there 10 years. Ten years too long, but I never expected her to legally file a motion for me to leave. That was a slap in the face and stab in the back. True, we had our ups and downs, but we were her only offspring. Aside from when we had a physical altercation where she bit me, this was another sign that something was going on. I'd been around my mom for 36 years, so I knew something wasn't right. Her behavior and mannerisms were changing. She was turning 70 that year, so in the back of my mind, I knew what was happening. I told both my baby daddies that the girls had to live with them until I found a place. If anybody was going to be homeless, it was going to be me alone. I'll be damned if I let my girls suffer with me.

So, I told them the situation and they went to stay with them until I got on my feet. Me and my 2nd baby daddy were no longer together and hadn't been for 2 years, and his ass still hadn't changed. I had to get a weekend job working midnights at another hotel while still working at the pharmacy full time during the week. I worked literally 7 days a week with no breaks because I had to make sure I had the money to come up with to find a place and maintain it. I don't think I lasted a full two months before this idiot told me he could no longer keep his kids. No legit reason, just he couldn't do it anymore. I had to quit my weekend job which I had no plans of doing until the summer time to make sure I had enough to make ends meet. He blamed not being able to keep the girls on his parents, claiming they were questioning him about my whereabouts and complaining about babysitting them, which I knew was bullshit. He just was incapable of responsibility, hence the reason we were no longer together.

I was even more mad because now he was fucking with my money, but luckily, I had made enough where I was able to put a deposit down for the home I found and be good for a few months, plus my tax refund had came, so I was also able to furnish my home with the basic necessities: the kids beds, a stove and refrigerator, washer and dryer, and lastly my bed. I even had enough left over to get a living room set. It took me almost two months to find a decent home for me and my daughters. I wanted something close to my mom and the girls' school and something that I could afford. I signed my lease in March, and moved in in April. The babies were back living with me, but my two oldest didn't come back until the school year was over. It only made sense since there were only two months left roughly.

That was one of the hardest decisions to make; not having all my babies with me and having them live with their dads. True, I could talk to them and visit them, but it's not the same when they've literally been with me 24/7 since they were in my belly. It wasn't long after we were officially moved out that my mom's health was declining. She was becoming mean and beyond disrespectful. I knew that she had some form of dementia and that it was only going to get worse. I didn't speak to my mom regularly because I was so hurt and confused as to why she did what she did, prior to her becoming more belligerent. When I did talk to her, she would cuss me out and call me everything but a child of God. There's only so much a person can take and I had had my fair share of disrespect.

I know that everything in life has a lesson behind it, good or bad, but most of the lessons are unexpected and quite painful. There's so much more of my story to tell, but these are just tidbits inside my world. I've already told most of my story in my memoir, but I may do another that elaborates more on what I've encountered in life. No, my life hasn't been traumatic like others, but that doesn't mean that I don't have a story to tell. We all do. Having to live the rest of your life with just one parent is hard. I know a lot of my peers didn't grow up with both parents, but I did. I was blessed to have my dad for as long as I did. I was a daddy's girl, and to see how these men abandon their kids willingly repulses me. Every child needs both their parents, but it's the parent's responsibility to raise their children.

We don't choose our parents and technically, parents don't choose their kids unless they're adopting. Knowing the bond that me and my dad had and knowing that there are kids, hell, even adults who lack that bond because the father wasn't ready or he just didn't want to be bothered or them and the mother are no longer together so the father says screw the kids too is sad. And yes, I know that there are mothers that shun their kids, but there are more fatherless homes than motherless ones. If I could have foreseen my future beforehand, I'd change half the things that I endured. But it honestly made me stronger, wiser, and a better person. I know that giving the benefit of the doubt is bullshit unless actions prove otherwise.

I should have left my two oldest dad alone and took his word for it when he said that he didn't want to be in a relationship because he had just lost his job and didn't know when he would be back on his feet. But me having the heart that I do, I saw past that. I've never been a gold digger or only dated guys with money. If you're trying to get yourself together, and working hard at doing so, then I could work with that. I don't feel that way anymore because you have to want to do better for your situation to change. I felt he wasn't trying hard enough. The amount of money you make should not overshadow the fact that if you're living with someone and using all their resources, including their vehicle, you should be contributing monetarily. Both my kids' fathers disrespected me at some time or another during our relationship and even after I broke things off with them because I was tired and knew I deserved better than what I was getting. They say watch what a man says when he's angry with you. It shows you how he truly feels about you. The words you say can either uplift someone or belittle them, so you have to choose your words carefully.

They both expected me to wait around for things

to change. I'd already wasted 8 years with one and 4 years with the other. How much time do you need to grow up, especially when there are kids involved and daughters at that. I know they don't want their daughters dating no loser guys, so they should be more cautious in how they move to make sure they set the best example of how a man is supposed to treat a woman. My heart is so big but has been tainted by false love and fakeness. I'm always the one to give and give and give and people always take and take and take. I never had an equally reciprocated relationship, not even friendships, except for the ones I cherish to this day.

My kids' fathers never appreciated me nor truly loved me. They used me to their convenience whether they knew it or not. And still, I'm the only sacrificer amongst parenting. I go above and beyond to make sure my babies have all of what they need and some of what they want, while they give the bare minimum. They get to go out and live their best lives, while I'm at home with no babysitter or having to nurse them back to health because they're sick from germs from school. I don't have freedom to do as I please because I always have to think of my kids first. I don't get to choose when I do and don't want to be a mother. I'm a mother 24/7/365 automatically. And despite all the wrongdoings I've ever had done to me, I'd never do anyone the way that I've been done. I was taught to treat others the way I want to be treated, but I never get treated that way. I get disrespected, embarrassed, and ridiculed. But one thing I will say about me, God has given me the strength to endure what I've been through and use this as a testimony to someday help others. I will remain strong and resilient. Only the strong survive, and only girls from the 'D' can do that.

Chapter Three

MEET NAYA PERRY-EDDINGS

I've always been a fan of "GO FOR IT" and no matter what, I've tried to live by it! Ima take you on a tour of my life. Hold on cause this roller coaster goes through some dark tunnels and muddy waters but comes out to the sun. Ima remind y'all about things as we go so when I say remember just think back.

Growing up on the streets of Detroit, as I look back.... Joy Rd is where you could find me! Single mom (Julia) and 1 brother (Mark). Mom did pretty decent if you ask me, working with what she had. I was around the Grand Parents, Aunts, Uncles, and Cousins who used to beat me up, lots of friends, and brought up in the church. (Let me tell you, if I knew then what I know now...Baby! Them church men...Shame.)

I attended the best grouping of schools McFarlane-Drew-MACKENZIE, in that order... Shout out to Class of 2000, The Dreamers. LOL. You know; the normal stuff. Throughout all the normal stuff I did, I never felt normal or that I fit in.

No matter how people see or view you, your inner thoughts are what really matters. I was a weird kid (so I was told.) Joining things is what I felt would make me fit in. I dressed different, I thought different, and I looked different! In Elementary school I suffered from "Split Personality Disorder" crazy right? All the way to high school I felt like the ugly duckling with low self-esteem. Why? I don't know, I just know that's how I always looked at myself. However, NOW Huni I'm like FINE WINE, I just get better over time! I still didn't know what I wanted to do in life, but I knew what I didn't want to do.

I did all the things a teen should do to experience being a kid growing up. Skipped school, got into fights, played sports, worked, went on dates. (By the way, I have two guys that I dated who had a BIG impact on my life that started in high school, Bobby Buckines and Aaron Walker. RIP to both and Thank You!) Graduation was approaching and I still have no idea what I wanted to do with my life. 'Trying to fit in is Crazy! Seems like torture! I guess I'll go to the military!'

The military, yes, good idea! I get to get away and

travel all while putting my life on the line for people who will never know me or ever care of my existence! Remember I said "GO FOR IT" yeah, this one of those moments. So away I go! Bootcamp yeah that's when I also started figuring out some more stuff I didn't want to do, "THIS Military CRAP" LOL. I stuck with it mostly because I had NO choice. During my tour on board USS Enterprise CVN 65 I escorted Robin Williams, Ben Affleck, and Donald Rumsfeld just to name a few. (I have pictures to prove it).

A host of Shipmates and BAYYBYY we got some stories!! (WE can talk about it when yall get ready). I did get to see the world. Oh, did you know I was in the battle group that did the bombing for 9/11 oversea? YEAH I've seen some things. They took me right over to harm's way. How dare they when I'm like fresh to the ship! Ohhhhhh sooo many stories I can tell. However, I retired out the military. I had a good run but I will NEVER do it again! I also Met the guy I THOUGHT I was going to build and be with forever. Turns out, that was a LIE! This is where the turn of events and easy life gets darkened. Now don't get me wrong Ima give him his props. Dude was gorgeous, Tall-ish, nice body, nice hands, good grade of hair, nice smile. I should have known it was too good to be true. I get it, all relationships go through tough times but Huni..... The Devil in human form.

Now I'm not going to go in all details but by the

grace of God I'm still here to tell the story of survival (if anyone wants to know the details.) Over the next 9 1/2 years, my faith, my trust, my mental, and my physical would be challenged. Yet it would all shape me to be who I am now! You wouldn't believe what I was put through. Not going to say that I was innocent but for every action there is a reaction. Ok, I'll give you an overview. This marriage was like MR. & MRS . Smith. I kid you not. Ask the neighbors!

There were holes in walls, tables broken, knives, fire, hospital stays, restraining orders, additional new babies coming forth, a living HELL!!! Finally, he had enough of me and kicked me and the kids out of the house. (which wasn't his, but ok). OMG! I want to go into more details but it would be a book for real! And now we are homeless, me and my 3 kids in Arkansas. What do I do? I have no family. Oh, and Arkansas is where he and all his family is from. Yet, no help! So, I guess... move into a shelter? So that's what I did. Ok, so he wasn't all to blame for the relationship but I had good reasons, right?!

Well, I had met this other guy a few weeks earlier at work, not with any intentions but I did meet him. Turns out he was right what I needed although I didn't know it at the time. My situation was getting worst and I needed to vent. I needed to leave. Since I was trying to leave the state, I messaged him. Since I wouldn't see him again, I gave him my back story and told him I was going to move back to Detroit. I told him it was because I was damaged goods and no one would understand what I've been going through. He handed me a stack of money to get out the shelter, get a place, and get my utilities on as long as I stayed for 2 years. So of course I agreed, I was already at my lowest.

At this point my faith was being restored. I wanted to be a part of giving back and helping people feel good about themselves because at that moment I felt like someone actually cared about me and my kids. Finally, I got a divorce and that's when I felt like I was getting back on track. Remember that guy I told you about, yeah, he stuck around for all of it. After my two-year agreement was complete, I moved back to Detroit (there's more to that as well)! Then, what do you know, two weeks later that guy came to visit me. We traveled back and forth visiting each other for 2 years. Shortly after I became extremely ill. With a bad case of ulcerative colitis and Classic shingles, and now suffering from internal nerve damage, (And that guy I told yall about put his life on hold to stay close by while I was hospitalized for 3 months). With the help of my Mom, Mark, Dorthia, Lisa and a few friends, I got better. Lord knows I was ready to give up. I had a talk with God and told him If he brings me out I would do better.

Now there is so much that I skipped. Not to say

it wasn't important. I might tell more later if you want but to continue... I got better and relocated to Charleston, IL. Detroit will always be home, just had to figure out what I could use to my advantage from there in another state (HUSTLE). That's what I'll do! I was looking for work and came across a post for a KJ- karaoke jock. Remember "GO FOR IT", so I did. I did great and 2 years later I got fired. Not for anything I did wrong but because the owner panicked and felt threatened (he told me this). He also told me I wouldn't amount to anything without him.

Of course I felt defeated. 2 months without working I got a call from a bar I did karaoke in (Joe's) telling me to get my stuff and be ready to work the following Friday. (Thanks Rachel Russell!)... and I'm still there doing what I do (oh yeah I bartend there as well currently). This is the change I needed. DJ Royalty was on the rise. I started doing more and my name got out there then I went from a nobody to famous in a small town. It's a great feeling. I started giving back and doing things in the community. People started asking me to DJ weddings. "GO FOR IT"! Don't get me wrong, I'm not the average DJ. I focus on the people. So, I don't do battles, but I get the job done. I started doing private parties, corporate parties, Proms, school dances, Repasses, you name it I probably done it!

When you lose yourself or the things that matter to you, you start moving different you think different eventually. I began doing things I never imagined doing I had an opening (and yes that guy I talked about, he was there giving the biggest support all while boosting my confidence, Remember I said "Fine as Wine" that was all him)! I decided to do more so I opened a food truck. WHATTTT?!?!?! Yeah. Did that and an event hall. Decided to form a social group for people who was away from their families (So we could support each other in the time of need). With the help of some key players, we made things happen. Don't think I didn't have a life while on my mission. I reconnected with my day 1, Shay Cole and I met my Day 2's here! Timarie N., Lelonna T., Brittany R, Danielle P, and LeeAnn S. I have 3 kids living with me Treveia, Tregion, & Treylin who are amazing in their own way and one of the reasons why I strive to do better (Oh I haven't gotten to talk about them yet. Oh my! Stand by! Cause now I have 9 kids)!

I've traveled with my friends and I've grown to love myself. Life is good. I still have the occasional mental issues but I'm working on them. In a town that has little to no growth I made way. I became the first African American to do a lot and get the recognition for it as a "PILLAR of the community!" The military taught me that I m not equipped to do just one or two things I was designed to multitask and do more. Make people feel good about themselves. "GO FOR IT"! When you feel like your whole world is falling apart you HAVE to keep on pushing.

In 2010, I was in a hit and run, if you saw my car, you would ask 'HOW did you walk away'. In 2014, I almost died from medical issues. In 2021, I had another brush with death. I passed out hitting my head on the corner of the display table in the middle of a store. Nonetheless, I'm here and still functioning. So when I tell my story to others, I don't want anyone thinking I'm bragging. I'm simply trying to let them know you can bounce back from situations that was intended to break you. I've been there and I feel like I deserve it all so I guess you can say I'm a hoarder of my lifestyle. "Hustler" I'm going to always want more for me and my family. That's because at one point I had NOTHING!

I'm not done doing things, I'm out to take over the world! I feel like my purpose in life is to make others feel good about themselves, laugh, and make life just a little bit easier. I discovered the reason why I always felt different is because I'm UNIQUE! I've been through so much trauma within myself that the average person would be sitting in the corner rocking and sucking their finger, or in the physciatric ward. My word of advice is "GO FOR IT"! Even if you fail at least you tried! Also, be kind. You never know who is going through things and who you will run into/need in the future.

Chapter Four

MEET SHANNON CAIN-WOMACK

I had a good life as my parents took good care of me and made sure that I didn't want for anything. I was surrounded by a loving family but mentally and emotionally I was becoming an emotional wreck. When they say don't judge a book by it's cover that means just that because you never know whats in the book until you read it. My life has been centered around some events that occurred during my childhood. For that reason I lived part of my life in fear, struggled with depression, and questioned my purpose and at times my existence. All of these barriers carried from my childhood well into my adulthood. Then there came a point in my life where I had to say enough is enough. It's time to set myself free. When people see me they see a happy person, someone who's full of life.

Which, yes that's me. What many people don't know is behind this smile and bubbly personality there's a hurt little girl who later became a grown girl crying.

I was just a nine year old innocent little girl doing what nine year old's do. I didn't know this one incident would affect my life in such a large way. My bookbag was heavy from my Lisa Frank trapper keeper and workbooks. As I ran I could hear were my pencils and crayons rattling around in my pencil box. My big heavy green coat came to my knees and was weighing me down. That didn't matter because I still managed to run for my life. I thought they were going to get us! I kept looking back and I saw them getting close. Yes, we were in the thick of winter but where was everyone? There wasn't a bird insight but feathers were flying!They were coming from what I called my imitation triple fat goose. The winter of 1991 changed my life. That nine year old little girl still lives inside of me.

First, let me start from where it all began; the winter of 1982 on February fifteenth. I was born at Hutzel hospital in the heart of Detroit City. Hutzel hospital was and still is where most babies were born especially if you were from the east side. I grew up hearing stories about Hutzel hospital. In fact I just knew that when I got older and had children I was going to have them where I took my first breath. When my mother birthed me, there were complications so I was unable to go home for almost a month after my birth. The intensive care unit was my home until then. I was born with a heart murmur, a common medical condition that meant I had a hole in my heart. In some cases it can be a very serious condition. In my case, I grew out of it in my later teenage years. Up until then I was monitored very closely by medical professionals.

From the beginning of my life I was faced with obstacles. After spending the first month of my life in the hospital's neonatal intensive care unit it was finally time for my parents to take me home. When I would got home, I was greeted by my brother (who's ten years my senior), my sister (who's seven years my senior), and lastly my parents pet dog Max (who would later on become my best friend). At the time my parents lived in a two bedroom two family flat on Baldwin Street. My brother and sister each had their own rooms and my parents turned one part of their house into a bedroom which was my room. I spent the first eight years of my life in that house until we moved on the same street approximately five houses down on the same side of the street.

My dad was a factory worker at Chrysler most of my life. He would work long hours to provide for his family. He was known in the neighborhood as the dog lover because of his love for dogs. I said my dad was a dog whisperer before the dog whisperer even came about. He's always been an animal lover. I grew up with frogs, turtles, snails, fish, cats, and dogs. We even had a pet duck. All of which he used to rescue from around the neighborhood. People used to stop by just to see our duck in amazement. Had I known any better I could have charged people one dollar each to see our pet duck as it was pure entertainment. With the money I made it would have been just enough for me to buy some chips, a juice, now-a-laters and a ring pop from the penny candy store that sat on Kercheval street.

Unfortunately one day our pet duck went missing. Let my dad tell it he was probably someone's Thanksgiving dinner, that's what he seems to believe. My dad made sure that when he took a trip to the store he was coming back with goodies for all the kids on the block. If the ice cream truck came around my dad was getting every kid on the block a neapolitan ice cream. He was born and raised in the City of Detroit in a part called "Black Bottom". He traveled many Detroit's roads and I was right there with him as a young child and throughout my life exploring the city. My mother was the family and neighborhood beautician. Graduating from cosmetology school she was known for doing the best jerry curls on the city's East side. Some even traveled from the West Side. For certain she had the whole east side of Detroit smelling like activor juice. By the time I was old enough Jerry curls were played out so I didn't get to wear one.

My brother was heavy into music. He and his friends would be in his room blasting the latest hip hop songs on his boombox and making beats. Therefore, at an early age I developed a love for music. He was also the neighborhood barber hooking all the young boys up with a high top fade or the gumby. For the first six years of my life I was my parents' baby girl. Then my parents got pregnant. I then had a baby brother who was born six days before my birthday. For the first two years of his life my parents celebrated our birthdays together until I was just too old to be celebrating with him. As I started growing up my sister took me everywhere with her and it wasn't because she wanted to, it's because my mother made her. I guess I was that annoying little sister.

My sister did all of her friend's hair so she made sure my hair was braided with different color beads with the foil at the end. My mother had the old heads in the neighborhood rocking a Jerry curl, my sister had the teen girls wearing spiral curls, feather ponytails, braids and crimps and boys in the hood rocked high top fades with crispy line ups looking eighties and nineties fresh because of my older brother. I also had three older sister's as well from my dad's previous marriage. Although we didn't grow up in the same household I would see them when they came to visit or their mom would let them get me on the weekends, something I looked forward to.

My family lived in close proximity to one another. My great grandmother and grandmother lived around the corner from us in some duplexes on Shipherd Street. My aunt's, uncles, and cousins were just a few doors down. When I was a kid I can remember the grown folk used to have a good old fashion time. My family had fun with the kids but when it was time for just grown folks us kids had to head in the room. I used to cry saying I wanted to be a grown folk. If I knew then what I know now I would have been running to that room happily. I lived in what you would call a tight knit community.

Our community was called down-a-way which is a subculture that extended over a stretch of blocks. We were a village, not only were we neighbors, we all became family. Everybody knew everybody. Until this day we still call it downaway and we're still family. Back in those days the village could chasize the kids without our parents getting upset or ready to fight. I better not dare think to do anything wrong because if one of my elderly neighbors saw me, my family was sure to know even before I hit the door because they were calling my parents on their landline. The grown-ups appreciated each other back in the day. I was the typical little girl. I loved being outdoors playing with my friend's, riding my bike in what we called a tunnel at Riverview Hospital, skating, jumping rope, playing tag, dodgeball, and playing all of the sweet hand games like zing zing zing.

I lived across from Butzel Recreation Center which was where my favorite park was located. I used to look forward to getting in the spaceships. You couldn't tell me I wasn't going to grow up to be an astronaut. I lived within walking distance of Belle Isle too so my dad would walk me there or we would ride bikes. Either way, the first thing I was doing was racing over to the big yellow giant slide. Which is where most of my bumps and bruises came from. I call them my war wounds. I loved it anyhow. There was no internet back then so I made my own fun with the other kids from downaway. Something this generation of kids are not too familiar with.

One of my most memorable childhood moments was when I was just eight years old. On June 28,1990 I got a chance to be in the presence of the great Nelson Mandella. He spoke at the old Tiger Stadium just after he was released from doing a twenty seven year prison sentence in South Africa. I remember the day clearly as I was with the summer camp that my mom had signed me up for that year. What a great experience I can actually say I saw Nelson Mandella. Although I had some terrible childhood experiences and memories I also have great memories as well. I miss my childhood, I thrive on nostalgia. Thinking about certain songs, looking at television shows, or eating my favorite childhood candy it gives me a feeling that warms my heart.

Bellevue Elementary School was the neighborhood school I attended. It was centered in the heart of a residential community in Downtown Detroit. I began Belleuve at three years old which was called head start. That was like a free grade since my birthday was after December first. I'm sure I enjoyed school then because it was all fun, naps, and snacks. As I began to get a little older I dreaded the thought of going to school. Sammy Davis Jr.'s "Hello Detroit" came on at 5:30 a.m. A local Detroit radio host played it every morning at the start of his show. That song became my alarm. That's how I knew that I only had one more hour left to sleep. Although I was happy to hear the song every day, I wasn't too thrilled about going to school. Not because I didn't want to learn but because I was bullied.

See, I was one of the biggest kids in my school as far as height and weight. By the fourth and fifth grade I was a taller than average, chubby little brown girl with long pigtails. I couldn't help that I was bigger than the average little girl but I still developed body image issues as a result. I maintained good grades then I started getting into trouble because I was defending myself from the bullies. The principal's and teacher's knew my mother and father on a first name basis and probably had our landline on speed dial for their convenience.

Let me go back to the frantic day. It was the winter of 1991. It was cold and the snow was tall. I'm not sure what happened but the walk home seemed different from most days. Instead of kids walking and running, racing to get home, there was no one. No kids waiting to get on the bus and no parents waiting for their kids. There were no dogs chasing kids home and no safeties directing kids across the street. It was like a ghost town as I can remember. It was an odd day, creepy to say the least. One that will change my life. A day I let taunt me for many years.

As my friend and I were walking, we started talking about our school day, how excited we were about hitting up the penny candy store, and about going out to play in the snow as we had been doing after school.

All of a sudden a gold, four door Honda Civic with three men inside pulled up alongside the street. One man was caucasian and two were African American. We kept walking not knowing what was coming next. After the car parked on the corner, two of the men got out of the car leaving the one man behind the wheel as the getaway driver. Then they began chasing us. In our pursuit to get away we were looking for anyone to help us but again it was deserted. There was no one to save us from these monsters. I just kept thinking they were about to get us as we continued to run through the big field.

I was so thankful there was snow on the ground because running through the mountains of snow made it difficult for the old men to keep up. Although my coat and bookbag made it hard for me to run, my friend and I still maintained a good pace while the old men were treading tirelessly through the snow. As we were running we kept looking for somebody, anybody who could help. Just when hope was faint, out of nowhere two of my older brother's friends appeared like angels. It seemed like they had fallen from the clear blue sky because where did they come from. No one was in sight for as far we could see. All I remember next is feeling relief.

Hysterically, we ran over to my brother's friends both screaming and out of breath. We tried but could barely get a word out. You could see the genuine concern that was painted on their teenage faces. They didn't know what was going on. Finally, we were able to get the words together and we told them what had just taken place. The men were still in pursuit but once they spotted the two teen boys they fled the scene at a high speed. My brother's friends walked my friend and I the rest of the way to my house.

As we approached my house all I was greeted with was the savory smell of fried Chicken being cooked. My mother came to the door as she heard the loud knock. The look in her eyes when she opened the door tells me she was confused as to why my brother's friends were bringing us home. My brother's friends began to tell my mother what happened and all she could do was hug me tight. She thanked my brother's friends for bringing us home. She called my friend's grandmother to tell her the news. My brother's friends were the real heros. They were just about eighteen or so at the time. I'm sure they didn't expect that at that very moment their mere existence would have been saving two little girl's.

I'm so thankful that when no one else was around God sent them out of nowhere like guardian angels. If it weren't for them we would have had nowhere to escape and it's possible you wouldn't be reading this now. Sadly, the following summer one of the teens lost his life on the same street he saved mine. When I found out about his death I was shocked. Not just because he saved my life but at that point, I hadn't even put the correlation together. He was like a big brother to me. He was my brother's friend and he was young. I didn't even really know about death then yet this hit close to home. His death was all over the news. There were protests and rallies held in his honor. My family and I were a part of it all. I will never forget him.

The other teen, now a fully grown man, is still alive. Maybe one day he'll get to read this story. That following year I graduated from Bellevue, I was in the fifth grade at eleven years old. My hair was in a big french roll and I had the spiral curls coming down on the side wearing a three piece olive suit that later turned into one of my Sunday's best church outfits. It looked like I had just graduated from middle school and not elementary. I knew the school's staff was happy to see me go but I was sad to leave them. I was even more sad when I knew some of my friends and I would never see each other again. Some lived across town and would be going to different junior high schools.

On the other hand I was happy to not see some people anymore, those people were my bullies. I moved away from my childhood street Baldwin in the summer of 1993. Just a few months before I was due to start Butzel Middle School. I wasn't too enthusiastic about the move, in fact I was devastated. Though we were still moving to Detroit I was moving away from my childhood friends across town. We had just graduated so we were excited to start our journeys as middle schoolers together. Instead I would be attending St. Raymond's, later to become Genesis, a Catholic school that sat diagonally across from my new home. We lived just a few blocks from 8 mile street. Not caring about the convenience of the location, it wasn't the school I wanted to attend. I didn't want to make new friends. I missed my childhood friends.

Dealing with separation anxiety that summer and nervous about starting school in the fall, I had a lot going through my mind. Not only was I dealing with those things specifically, I also had to deal with the fact that my childhood dog Max had run away about three weeks after we moved to our new house. Max and I grew up together. He was truly my best friend. He was the first animal I've ever loved. I can definitely say he left his mark on me. When people ask me about the scar on my lip I explain the story just as it happened.

I was four years old running around the house playing with Max, as I always had. I decided to go to the bathroom to get a brush so that I can brush Max's tail. He was a German Shepherd so he was big with a big tail. As I began brushing his tail he was trying to get away from me but everywhere he ran, I ran. Suddenly he turned around and bit my upper lip splitting it open. It was stitched up but still to this day the scar is visible. For some reason I believe Max traveled back to our old neighborhood when he ran away. I just wished he took me back with him.

I started to meet some of the kids from around the neighborhood and I began to adjust well. Growing up in my old neighborhood it was predominantly African American. When I attended Bellevue school it was only one Caucasian student and his mother worked at the school. So being around all nationalities was new for me. One that I can appreciate because I began to learn about diversity. I was the new girl on the block so of course there were still kids that teased me because of my size but that didn't last long. I wasn't really too worried. I was accustomed to it and was ready to defend myself if need be.

It was 1994 I completed my first year at my new school and I was going to the seventh grade. That's when things began to change for me. During this time, news broke out of a missing four year old boy who was kidnapped while out shopping with his mother. This story made not only the local news but also the national news. Eventually I became obsessed with watching the coverage of this missing little boy. I needed to know every detail. I wanted him to be found alive.

While watching the continuous news updates of the missing toddler that then caused my mind to go back to a few years prior recalling what I could remember about the kidnapping and murder of a missing little girl. I remembered bits and pieces of her story. It was May of 1992 a ten year old little girl was taken away from her parents tragically. She was abducted while at a sleepover. As I proceeded to piece together the details that I could remember of this young girl. I couldn't believe someone would do this to an innocent little girl. Now there I was thinking about the kidnapping and murder of a ten year old girl that occurred two years prior and the recent disappearance of the toddler boy.

I continued on with my obsession with the story of the missing boy. As the days went on I began to think about my own attempted adduction. The thoughts were starting to move front and center in my brain. I began to have flashbacks of that day more and more. At twelve years old I realized that these men meant us no good and that was what I didn't understand at nine. There it was, the repressed memories started to rear their ugly head. The same thing that happened to that little girl could have happened to me. At this point, I was just praying for the safe return of the baby boy.

I was in the eighth grade getting ready to complete my last year of middle school. I still maintained good grades, if nothing else I took my school academics seriously. However, I stayed in trouble and was suspended from school often because of my antics. I was known around the school as being a clown. I went to school every day to entertain. I loved to make people laugh, and still do now. Somehow I managed juggling being the school's funniest person and still receiving good grades. I don't know how but it worked. On the flip side, most times after school I would go home and hibernate in my room. I wasn't coming out unless it was for the basic essentials and to go to school. Consumed with constant thoughts of my attempted kidnapping, I tried to divert my attention by picking up a pencil and a sketch book and beginning to draw.

I didn't know what I was drawing, I was just drawing. That's was when I discovered that I could draw, so

I used drawing as a way of expression and to occupy my mind. My parents were flabbergasted at the talent I didn't even know was buried within me. Even though I was starting to put together the puzzle of my life, there were still some missing pieces. I didn't think of everything all at once. The memories, thoughts, and questions were coming to me in bits and pieces. It wasn't really until age sixteen when I was attending Finney High School, that I was offered an opportunity to take a college psychology course to receive a college credit. Not only was it a great opportunity academically, it was going to give me more insight on the mind and its processes. I was hoping it was going to help me understand why at sixteen I was still being affected by memories from when I was nine.

After reading the course summary I went straight to my high school counselor's office to sign up for the Saturday psychology class that was held at Wayne State University. I needed some understanding. I needed to know why. Why now were the memories of that nightmare continuously taking over my mind? Was I triggered by those other two situations that I saw in the news? As the time went on I became even more engulfed with the thought of being kidnapped. I live with vivid memories of the day replaying in my head like it's on repeat. I kept envisioning my parents standing over a casket with my young body, crying while I layed there, looking as if I was peacefully sleeping in a pretty pink dress.

Throughout my life I continued to study psychology, even choosing it as my college elective. I gained an even deeper understanding and became even more knowledgeable in the subject. "Unexpressed emotions will never die. They are buried alive and will come forth later in uglier ways" (Sigmund Freud). Repressed memories are real. I unconsciously disassociated myself from the event until I was old enough. Now, later on in life these repressed memories would affect my adulthood even to this day. This situation for me had a very negative impact on my life. The depression, anxiety, and fear has had me in shambles. I was already battling insecurities about my body and the way I looked, in a nutshell I disliked myself.

If anyone would have asked me what I liked about myself that would have been an easy answer, nothing at all. I spent most of my life complaining about my weight talking down on myself. Talking myself out of doing things because I was consumed with fear. I didn't have the confidence to do anything. Yes, I was a class clown and entertainer in middle school and I played volleyball but I was still withdrawn. No one would have ever thought that I was dealing with such heaviness in my heart. I was taught not to question God because he didn't make mistakes.

My mother drilled that in my head but as much as she drilled it I wasn't hearing it. I was perplexed about my life's purpose. I didn't know why I was put on this earth. I wondered why I was here to suffer when my life could have just ended at age nine. I've encountered many obstacles. Things that were easy for others were never easy for me. Yes, I'm aware that not all things are meant to come easy but why was everything so hard for me? When you hear the statement one out of ten, I'm usually that one of ten.

Just A few years back around 2018 to be exact. I was sitting in my living room home alone. I remember the day like it was yesterday. I had just got home from work at the time I was working as a home health aide. It was a beautiful, sunshine filled, summer day. Fresh out the shower I sat in silence unwinding from my work day. The question arose as it would often. What is my purpose? Right then and there a still voice whispered gently in my ear "You are here to help others." It's something about that still voice. I pondered on this question throughout my life and now it has been answered. We ask questions that sometimes we may not get the answer to until years or so down the line and this was the case for me. At that very moment I felt a sense of relief. I now know that I'm here not just for myself, I was also here to help others. It all was coming together. Helping others is exactly what I did. Right then and that very moment I went into the time machine. As I began to reminisce about how I became interested in caring for others and looking back on some experiences in my life, my mind began to drift.

Let me rewind back to April the year of 1995, I was thirteen years old, in seventh grade. My grandfather, my dad's father, suffered a stroke. When he got out of the hospital he went into a nursing facility. I would go frequently to see my grandfather as my dad went to see him everyday, sometimes even twice a day. My grandfather wasn't getting the care he needed at the facility he was in so my dad transferred him to a different facility. I would just sit and observe and look at the older people. Some were surrounded by their families and some just sat alone. My heart would be full of grief every time I stepped foot in that place. It was sad. All I can remember is the smile that came across my grandfather's face whenever he saw me walk in the room.

It made my heart smile as tears filled my eyes. Sadly, my grandfather passed that same year in April of 1995. I was crushed, my heart was shattered in a million pieces. Not my grandfather. I didn't know how I was going to go on. I became consumed with grief not to mention seeing my dad hurt made it even worse. I'll never get over the death of my grandfather. If I didn't know anything else I know he loved me dearly. His smile when he used to see me is one of the memories I hold close to my heart. The day's went on and I mourned his death. I began to take it one day at a time. Until one day not long after my never mended heart would be shattered again.

My beloved grandmother, my mother's mother, came to stay with us just about a few months before the passing of my grandfather in 1995. She was living with us at the time of my grandfather's passing. My grandmother was ill so I would assist my mother with caring for her. Helping bathe, feed, comb her hair, and even doing her nails. She had home health care so nurses would come to care for her as well. I was intrigued with watching the nurses, I sat and observed everything they did for my grandmother. I was in the seventh grade and I had an assignment which was to interview someone in an occupation that we may be interested in when we are older. Automatically my first thought was to interview one of the nurses that came to see my grandmother.

After I conducted the interview I changed my occupation from wanting to become a veterinarian to becoming a registered nurse. I loved my grandmother dearly so I did whatever I had to do to help care for her. I hated the fact that my grandmother was sick and there was nothing I could do about it. As the weeks went on my grandmother became even more ill. I had just months prior lost my grandfather. I couldn't lose my grandmother too. My 13 year old heart couldn't handle yet another heartache. My routine was to go straight to my grandmother's room to make sure she was okay and tell her about my day.

This one particular day my routine felt different. The Catholic school that I attended was right across the street so it took me three minutes to get home. I had a school field trip as it was nearing the end of the school year. We went to an outdoor adventure park and I had a blast. I remember the day as if it were yesterday. It was a nice beautiful day. I was happy I had just had fun at the park so I couldn't wait to go home to tell my grandmother all about my trip. When I went in the house I felt something was wrong. It felt weird. It was quiet, you could hear a pin drop. When I went to my grandmother's room instead of happiness I felt sadness. My grandmother was laying in the bed just looking at the ceiling. Usually she would be happy to see me but this day it's as if I didn't exist.

She didn't know I was there. My Mother came into the room and saw the look of grief and confusion on my young face. She hugged me tight. Minutes later I heard the loud sirens as the EMS would arrive to take my grandmother to the hospital. When they left with her, little did I know that would be the last time I would see her. My grandmother passed away. Just like that I lost my grandfather, my dad's father in April of 1995 and my grandmother my mom's mother June 1995. Both whom I loved dearly. I went through a wave of emotions during this time with losing my grandparents, talking about grief stricken that was an understatement. Now I had two parents grieving over the loss of a parent and there was nothing I could do but let both my parents know I loved them.

Things for me just didn't seem normal, it all felt like a dream. The only problem was that it wasn't. With the back to back deaths of my grandparents, I begin acting out. My dad bought my mom a brand new 1994 Duster right after we moved and I used to itch to drive it. That Duster was a step up from the 'K' car we had! One day the opportunity presented itself when my sister was in a supermarket on East 7 Mile. The biggest mistake she could have made was leaving the keys in the car. I decided to get out of the car, walk around to the driver seat, and close the door. I started the car and it began to roll through the parking lot. I didn't know the brake from the gas so I didn't have my foot on either. There was a residential street directly across the street from the supermarket so I slowly rolled right across the parking lot and slammed into a parked car.

My seventeen year old sister was driving and I thought it was cool. Yet at that moment, I knew I had messed up. Without hesitation I got out and fled the scene. I was running like a football player with a football tucked in my arms racing for the touchdown! I didn't stop till I was at my cousin's house. I told her what happened and I hid in her closet for hours. I was begging for snacks in the closet and crying at the same time. I knew it was a wrap once I was located. By night time my mother found out where I was and I went home. When I got home I was scared to walk through the door because I didn't know which wall I was going to be knocked into or which tooth my mother was going to knock out first. I didn't know what to expect.

When I went in the house my mother couldn't even look at me. My dad worked the afternoon shift so I knew I better go get some shut eye because when he got home I knew I had a whooping coming. Just when the sleep was getting good I saw the light turn on through my eyelids and I knew it was time. My dad whooped me good! He didn't beat me but he made sure it was good enough for me to still feel it today!

By the way, that was my last whooping ever. Looking back on that experience, I realize that the accident could have turned out to be all bad. I often have flashbacks on that day because I blacked out and I didn't have a clue what to do. I think about had the car been faced the opposite way I would have rolled head on in the traffic on seven mile street. That was truly a fight or flight moment and I did the latter. My life was spared and it s all by the grace of God that I'm alive to tell this story. Not only were my parents still grieving their parents, but they could have been burying me as well. This incident was all tied to my purpose. I was meant to be here. I have a purpose to fulfill.

When social media came out I used to search for my friend, the girl I was with the day of our attempted kidnapping. Years later she eventually popped up on my friends list. When I saw her I added her as a friend immediately. When she accepted my friend request I sent her a message right away. I needed to ask her if she remembered that awful day. I needed to know if her life was affected by the incident like mine. To my surprise when I read the answer to my message I was floored. Her answer was no, no she did not remember the incident. I couldn't understand for the life of me how I was so affected by this and here it turns out that she didn't have any recollection of that day at all. That just goes to show that certain things and situations affect people differently.

To date my two greatest blessings are my beautiful daughter's. I first became a mother in the Winter of

2003. I was in my junior year living in the new on campus apartment at Oakland University. I found out I was pregnant with my daughter one month after my twenty-first birthday. I thought I couldn't have kids because my husband, then boyfriend, and I were together for six years before we conceived. Not that we were trying. One day my best friend who was also my roommate and I were walking around campus getting some exercise in and I felt a pain in my side. Stopped at a red light as we were getting ready to cross the street. I told my friend that maybe we should turn around because I wasn't feeling right. The next day I made an appointment with my physician. When I got to the doctor's office the first thing they did was give me a pregnancy test. In the back of my mind I'm thinking for what.

When the doctor came back into the room she said do you know that you are pregnant? My mouth dropped! Not because I was upset but because I just wasn't expecting her to tell me that. I went on to live on campus until it was time for me to deliver her. She actually made it to the end of my junior year. My second pregnancy was not a live birth. In 2005 I found out I was pregnant. This time I knew for sure. I was six weeks pregnant when I found out however this time things were different. We were in the middle of planning our wedding which was set for October 22, 2005. When I found out we were pregnant we moved the wedding up to July 30, 2005.

One day I was walking in the park with my daughter

and I felt a sharp pain. I was scared so I proceeded to stroll my daughter back to the car. When I got back home and went to the bathroom I was bleeding. Immediately I panicked. I told my husband, then fiance, what was going on and in no time I was headed to the hospital's emergency room. Cramping and spotting I knew that wasn't a good sign. Called back into the room I was given an ultrasound that showed the sac but the baby was nowhere to be found. With a second ultrasound done a baby was detected on the ultrasound. For almost 2 months I was back and forth to the doctor's office for blood work. I went in for another ultrasound, as it had become my routine, and that's when they broke the news to me that there indeed was no baby. I was heartbroken yet again.

I was pregnant with the sac that was still keeping up with the gestation. I was instructed to schedule an appointment at the hospital for dilation and curettage (D&C) which is the removal of tissue in the uterus. Within the next few days I was going in for the procedure. I was nervous, honestly I was ready to get it over with. The whole ordeal was stressful and an emotional rollercoaster. We proceeded with the wedding plans shortly after my procedure. Our wedding continued on as planned on July 30, 2005. Which was two months after my miscarriage. After the wedding we went to Pontchartrain in Downtown Detroit where we celebrated our nuptials. That's also when our baby girl was conceived. She was born in the Spring of 2006.

I actually can say she was truly a honeymoon baby.

God blessed us with her right after the miscarriage of our angel, whom I believe was my baby boy. I knew once I had children, especially daughters, I was going to be a bit overbearing. I wanted to protect them from what I went through. I didn't want any men looking at my daughter's the way those terrible men were looking at me. When we went anywhere I had a panic attack when they drifted off. Honestly, I'm still that way with them. I rarely used to let my daughters go to anyone's house for a sleepover. When I did it took a long time for me to allow them to do it. I just didn't trust people. With memory of an innocent little girl being taken from her friend's house during a sleepover looming in my mind, I was very leary. Although it wasn't a recent event, it was substantial. At the same time, I was trying not to be frustrated with the children for not understanding. I reiterated to them my reasoning and always reminded them of what almost happened to me. I was not going to let it happen to them.

Well, after the death of my beloved grandparents, I kept the promise that I made to myself. I decided I was going to go into the medical field. I wanted to take care of people. Although I went to college after high school, I didn't go into nursing. Ideally, I still wanted to become a registered nurse. However, It wasn't until 2007 when I decided that I wanted to enroll in a 9 month course to become a Medical Assistant. After graduating from the program I received my certificate and began my internship at a doctor's office working their front and back office. In 2009 I accepted a job at an adult foster care working with men with special needs. I held that job down for almost two years before I enrolled in a course to become a Certified Nursing Assistant.

Still at the adult foster care I took on a second job in a skilled nursing facility after I completed my program. When I started my job in the skilled nursing facility the experience was much different than the adult foster care. Instead of taking care of just a few people in a home-like setting I was in a building that housed a few hundred people. So the number of people I would care for in a single shift would double. I shadowed someone for the first week and on my very first day one of her residents passed away. Going into the field I knew it was bound to happen. I just wasn't expecting for it to happen on my first day. For a moment I had second thoughts. I stuck with it for sometime.

One of the most rewarding feelings is when I would go to work and there was a caring heart waiting for me at the nurses stations. A caring heart was a pendant recognized for good service. The only way one could get a caring heart is by filling out a form stating why a caregiver was getting this heart. Not only did I get them from my resident's family, I received them from nurses as well. It was the best feeling ever. I loved my residents! So to see them smile when I came in to work every day let me know that I was doing something right. I knew that I would be a great caregiver. It was my goal and I was going to make sure that I lived up to it. I'm not going to say it's easy caring for people because it isn't. No one really talks about the mental effect caregiving can have on someone.

I went home crying many days and nights thinking about the residents that would pass. It was draining. Everyone can do it yes but if you don't have compassion the healthcare field isn't just for anyone. I've been sensitive and compassionate my whole life. It was like a gift and a curse now I just see it as a gift. This takes me back to the day in 2018 when I was sitting in my living room when I asked God what my purpose was and the still voice said "Your purpose is to take care of people" it was all making sense. From that very day I never asked what my purpose of existing was. In 2021 and 2022, I went through a rough time in my life. I dealt with the deaths of friends and family during this time. It was literally one thing after another. I didn't know where to turn or what to do. Most days I didn't know if I was coming or going.

During this time I spent a lot of moments alone and started taking myself out to dinner or lunch, which I had never really done before. I begin to enjoy the company of myself and getting to know me because I never really knew me. Surprisingly there's a lot of people who don't really truly know themselves. As I spent more and more time with myself I began to deal with some of the issues that I had I faced throughout the years. Even though I was getting to know myself, God placed some special people in my life during these tough years. For that I'm thankful because he knew these people were meant to be in my life. I'm a firm believer that everybody comes into our lives for a reason. Over the course of this time I began to challenge myself by taking on different things that I would have otherwise talked myself out of. I feel I would have been a lot further in life had I not lacked the confidence to do the things I wanted to do. I was going through a transformation at the time I didn't realize it. I wanted to be a model for a long time. I talked about it passionately for many years but I was too nervous and ashamed. I didn't want everyone to treat me like I was Carrie and laugh at me.

I used to tell people that I was an aspiring model. Now I can actually say that I am a plus size model. I really can't describe with words the feeling that I have when I say that. I allowed my lack of confidence to hold me back for many years. As a teenager I prayed that I would have the courage to actually put myself out in the modeling world. Instead of having fashion shows and photoshoots in my head. I am now participating in professional photoshoots. I no longer live that dream in my head. I'm coming out so the world can see what's been hiding inside of me. The irony of me modeling is that I was once bullied for the way I looked but I turned that negative situation into a positive. I feel great about myself now and I'm loving it.

Everything I once disliked about myself I'm now finding beauty in. I just wished it hadn't taken me so long to discover but this is God timing. Also during that time I learned that I would become a grandmother. The news came in August of 2022 while at the doctor with my daughter. Although I was in a dark space, just knowing that my grand child was soon to come gave me something to look forward to. I didn't get a chance to have a boy but I thank God for blessing me with my grandson who was born in March of 2023. Which is one of the best days of my life, witnessing the birth of my first grandchild. I've always heard people talk about that grandparent/ grandchild love and how there was something special about it. I love my grandson so much and now I see why my love for my grandparents was so deep. Oh how I miss my grandparents.

This book, *Just A Girl From Detroit,* is one of my biggest accomplishments to date. It was the beginning of 2023. One morning I was just waking up and I had a message. When I opened it, I was beyond speechless. My former college mate friend, and sister asked me if I'd be interested in participating in this collaboration. I didn't think twice before I said "Yes"! I had something to prove to myself. I wasn't going to turn back now which was something that I had acquainted myself with doing. In the past, no matter how bad I wanted to do something, I just didn't have the courage. Not this time! I was going to complete this piece. Just as I had overcome my fear of modeling, I was going to conquer the fear of telling my story. The effects of my childhood have taken up enough of my energy.

I really didn't know what I was up against. I cried

a lot of tears during this process. I was walking my dog one day and I asked why I was chosen for this assignment. Suddenly I heard, "Stop asking why you were chosen, just be thankful that I chose the right person to choose you". It's something about hearing that still voice. When I was chosen to do anything good I thought to myself this person must have made a mistake by choosing me. Simply put, I just didn't believe that I was worthy of such opportunities. Like I mentioned previously, I talked myself out of so many opportunities. I'd say yes to something and then I'd find a way to back out of it. It wasn't because I didn't want to do those things, it's because I was too fearful and didn't want to fail. I believed my entire life that I was undeserving of anything good to happen for me that when it did I was surprised. Since everything went wrong for me, that's what I started to expect. I was so blinded by the false reality that I created of myself that it was hard to see anything good. This is a learned behavior that I'm slowly but surely unlearning.

During the process of writing "*Just a Girl From Detroit*". I decided to go visit the corner field of my attempted adduction. I call it a corner field because it's a big field on the corner. I was talking to my husband one night and I was crying. I looked at him and said 'I want to go visit the spot'. He didn't even have to ask me where because he already knew. I had an up and coming appointment in that area the following week so I knew we would be passing by the street. He was okay with going with me; he just wanted to make sure I was going to be able to handle it. The following week was now here and in just a few days I would be going to visit the same spot I was almost abducted.

My anticipation began to grow stronger. I wasn't changing my mind, there was no turning back and now I was ready to go. When we pulled up to the location I immediately started looking around scoping the scene. It was a beautiful sunny Saturday morning. The air was fresh and no one was outside. I was back in ghost town. I instantly started having flashbacks. I got out first leaving my husband to park. When we got out of the car I began to relive the entire incident giving my husband a play by play on every detail. Then my husband got back in the car as I just wanted some time to stand there in the field alone.

I began feeling as if my adult self was waiting for my nine year old self to come running so I could rescue her. I pictured myself telling her that it wasn't her fault that she was just a little girl. I would hug her tight and tell her she deserves happiness, she is worthy of good things happening to her, she doesn't need to live in fear, it's okay to be different, and what could've happened to you didn't happen. As those thoughts of what I would tell my nine year old self filled in my head, my eyes were filled with tears and they started pouring down like a water fountain. I never thought to actually visit the site because I knew it would be difficult but I'm glad I did because I felt a sense of peace. It was as if I was releasing everything I was feeling throughout the years. It was a huge relief.

Sometimes we have to go back to that painful place and that's just what I did. Over the course of writing, I thought about my life from beginning to end and that was painful. It's like I'm playing in a movie and I'm the starring character in my own life's story. My eyes did a lot of crying and my heart was heavy for many days and nights. I was becoming uncomfortable with some of the things that I was thinking about. Not all things are not meant to be comfortable. I spent many days and nights not wanting to pick up my notebook and pen. It wasn't because I didn't want to write, it was because I knew that I was going to have to think about some painful things. It feels as if I've lived many lives in my lifetime as I've been through a lot of different experiences.

That's why I have to come to terms with all of the challenges that I've faced. They were only preparing me for moments such as this. If I didn't go through anything there wouldn't be anything for me to share with others who may be going through or who have gone through what I've been through. I know that I am chosen. I know that I have a calling on my life and now it's time for me to ascend and rise to the call. I know I can't erase any of my memories. What I can say is that now I have a new perspective on things that I've encountered in my life. The ugly parts of my past is what made me the woman I am today. I won't be embarrassed about any of it.

Every obstacle that I've ever encountered in my life I can honestly look back on each one and I'll be able to pick the blessing as well as the lesson that I got from them. I now recognize that not every trial and tribulation was not meant to destroy me, they made me stronger. God gives the toughest battles to the toughest soldiers and I'm a soldier. From the beginning of my life as you can see the odds were against me but my steps were already ordered even before I was created. That's why everything that came to harm me didn't prosper. My life was spared several times and it was all because of God's grace and mercy. Whilst I was complaining about the obstacle courses I've been through, they were all tied to my purpose and I want to live a purpose driven life. People deal with trauma differently. How I dealt with my trauma may be different from how the next person deals with their trauma. Not everyone is going to have the same story. Nevertheless, we can all learn from someone else's pain.

For a long time I knew that I wanted to share my story. I know I'm not the only one going through childhood traumas and its after effects. I did my own research on dissociated memories but not everyone is aware. I'm not preaching but I wouldn't be able to talk about it if I didn't go through it. I'm thankful for this opportunity because I'm finally getting a chance to share my story. This is a part of my healing journey. "There is no greater agony than bearing an untold story inside of you" (Maya Angelou).

For many years I questioned why me. Why did they want to do this to me? I had questions but no answers until recently. Why not me? I finally realized after all of these years that this devastating ordeal happened for a reason. And one thing that I'm a firm believer of is that everything happens for a reason. It was all part of the process. A lot of times we hear people say trust the process but do we really know what that means? At this stage in my life I'm finally trusting the process. I wish I could go back to some situations where I should have trusted the process. One thing about life is it'll surely show you some things but it's up to us to learn from them.

My story is just beginning. I don't know who this is going to reach but I pray that it reaches someone who has struggled with fear, body image issues, someone who felt like they weren't good enough, someone who suffers from childhood trauma, someone who suffers from depression and anxiety. Whomever it reaches, just know that you are not alone, don't suffer in silence. It took me until now to realize that people can't make me happy; they can only add to my happinesses. Today, I'm not going to say I'm one hundred percent healed from my childhood traumas because I'm not. I wouldn't be honest with myself or you. How can I expect others to be honest with me if I'm not honest to myself first? Being bullied as a kid took a toll on my mental health.

I can relate to why kids commit suicide as I had a few failed attempts. But God. Moving forward I'm choosing to change my perspective on the whole attempted kidnapping incident. I let the what ifs control my mind and my life for so long. I am no longer focusing on the idea that I was could've been murdered and dumped somewhere like a rag doll. I'm focused on the fact that I am still alive. I'm alive here today sharing my story and my experience and how I've gotten to the point I am today. I still have a lot of living to do and a lot more things to accomplish. I don't know where this is going to lead me but one thing for certain I can say is that I'm ready. For the first time in my life I'm trusting the process. I never really been proud of myself but today I can say I am extremely proud of myself and I'm clapping for me.

I'm going to continue doing the things I love, which is spending time with my family, listening to music, dancing, traveling, modeling, and I'm going to continue pursuing writing. We have to make a choice to do the things needed to heal in order to reach true happiness for ourselves. I'm still a work in progress. I still have a lot more healing to do because that is what I have chosen to do. Counseling has been very beneficial for me. I'm going into a new season in my life. I wouldn't change anything that I've been through for the world. I'm right where I am supposed to be in my life at the moment. I'm not quite where I want to be but I'm far from where I used to be. And I can't wait to see where I'm headed. I may have thought everything I went through was all bad while I was going through it. But in reality looking back on it, the obstacles in my life were necessary for my growth. Without any of these experiences I wouldn't have learned so many valuable lessons and most importantly I wouldn't have a story to share to help encourage others. One thing for sure, two things for certain, I am not ashamed of where I've come from or the things that I've been through. I'm from the East Side of Detroit! Some would have called it the ghetto but I call it home, it's where I was born and raised. No matter where I end up in life I'm forever going to be, "Just a Girl From Detroit". Where only the strong survive.

Chapter Five

MEET SHAY COLE

It was Friday, January 15, 1982, when I came sliding into the world. Marlene and Robert Tyus, my parents, decided to have a baby together after they both had a few before they met. My mom had three and my dad had seven. They thought I was a boy before I was born so they were gonna name me Martin Luther, since I was due on Martin Luther King Junior's birthday. To their surprise, a seven pound eleven ounce baby girl was born. My mom's childhood friend, Onga, was the person who actually named me Shaquanda. I remember asking my mom about how I got my name. When she told me she didn't name me, I was appalled! I mean my siblings had decent names and I felt that my name was so ghetto, even at an early age. When she told me she wasn't the culprit and that it was her friend who had actually changed her name to Onga, I was disappointed. I couldn't believe my momma went along with that. However, here I am. A real life Shaquanda.

My mom didn't have any girl names for me since she thought I was a boy. So that's how she ended up giving the task to her friend. My mom still wanted to honor Martin Luther King in some way since I was indeed born on his birthday. So she gave me the middle name Marie. My mom and dad were married a little while before I was conceived and they were divorced before my first birthday. Although they ended their marriage, they remained great friends and co-parents. My parents both worked in the factory for most of my early childhood. My mom was a seamstress at Ford and my dad worked at General Motors, not sure what he did. When I was around nine, my mom had to have heart surgery and I had to go stay with my dad. It was kinda bitter-sweet because I was used to walking to school with my friends.

I lived on Pinehurst and Joy with my mom and went to school based on her address. For elementary school I attended McFarlane on Joy and Cheyenne. My dad lived on Wyoming Ave near the Jeffries Fwy. He had a massive garden and farm at one point. So when I stayed with him, I had to get driven to school and he always listened to gospel hymns and gospel talk radio. My dad was 45 when I was born so when he dropped me off my friends would ask me if he was my granddad because he looked so old compared to their parents. While my mom was recovering, I could only visit her until it was ok for me to come home. I was so worried about her. We didn't have the best relationship but I yearned to please her and to make her happy. When I saw her hurting, I knew she wasn't happy. The only thing that really cheered me up when I was feeling sad at my dad's house was my friend Pie. Her grandma stayed next door and we quickly became the best of friends after we met. When she wasn't around, things were that much harder to deal with.

In 1993, both of my parents got new vehicles. Ironically, they also both got red vehicles. My mom got a Ford Thunderbird and my dad got a GMC Sierra. I was happy about both but I was super excited about my dad's because he had my initials, SMT, hand painted on the doors above the handles. So every time I rode in the truck I felt like it was really my truck. Some of my fondest memories with my dad are the road trips we took to Tennessee every year. I always looked forward to getting out of school for the summer to be able to hop in the truck with my dad and hit the highway. I was his road buddy. He even went so far as to put a camper top over the bed and put a twin size mattress back there for me to relax and get comfortable during the ride. I was his baby girl and he didn't play no kinda games about me. I remember him and my mom talking to me one day and telling me that he was offered a job in Texas but he turned it down for me. That resulted in his early retirement from General Motors.

I believe I was in middle school around this time. I loved my middle school! I went to Charles R. Drew! We had so much fun in class. That's where I was introduced to DAPCEP and eventually the ASPIRES program. I guess you could say I was kinda smart. I do remember having to do a project in English class one time and we had to have partners. My partner was the smartest girl in the school. I knew our project was going to be great. There was this one student that everyone was anxious to see. I believe his name was Aaron. When he presented his project to the teacher she screamed and sent him to the Principal's office. Before he could leave out someone revealed that Aaron actually had brought in live roaches as apart of his project. There were tons of funny moments like that and tons of fights too. I was involved in a few myself. My first fight was actually in 3rd grade with this boy named Andre Adams. He did not care that I was a girl cause he punched me dead in my eye.

From then on, I only fought boys. I remember this boy named Adam kept throwing crayons across the room at me in class one day. I told him to stop but he didn't listen. I then proceeded to warn him that if he continued down that path, I would have no choice but to get up and slap fire out his face. I guess Adam had his lucky draws on that day because he rolled the dice and kept on throwing crayons. Now, the teacher is in the room watching this. If I'm not mistaken it was Mrs. Brown's class. He threw one crayon across the room and it hit me. Not only did it hit me, it struck me in the eye. I politely moved my desk away from me and walked towards him and followed through with my promise. I slapped him so hard he came out the desk. He was mad and put me in the headlock so I started punching him in the back of the head. Then the teacher wanted to get involved. I mean, I wasn't too mad cause I didn't get in trouble. She said she watched me tell him to stop and warn him so he got what he deserved. That was usually how it went when I got into it with boys. They always felt like I would back down because I'm a girl and I am not backing down! Especially when you doing something to me.

I had a short fuse. I had already been through so much and felt like I had to constantly defend myself so that's what I did. Until one day something happened that I couldn't protect myself from. My mom would go to my oldest sister every Saturday to get her hair done. At this particular time, my great grandma and my grandma was living with us. It was a Saturday morning and I was awakened by my great grandma on the phone telling someone that my sister had died. I was so confused and irritated all at the same time. I told my great grandma to stop saying that because it wasn't true then I grabbed the house phone and started calling people. I called my mom, she didn't answer. I called my oldest sister, she didn't answer. I called my sister that my great grandma was talking about and she didn't answer. At this point I'm freaking out. I couldn't do my chores like I would usually do on Saturday because I was inundated with fear and confusion. Then, a few hours later, I heard the side door open. I ran down the stairs from my room and stood at the threshold waiting to see my sister walk through the door. I heard laughter and saw my mom first. Then I saw my godmother and my dad. It was when I saw my oldest sister that I knew.

Once I saw her, I fainted. I completely blacked out. I remember waking up sitting on the floor and going off. I don't remember getting all the details, I was just told that she was at her baby daddy's house and she was shot. I knew there was something more to the story but I was only 13 at the time and every time I tried to speak up or demand answers, I was silenced. I tried to figure out the full puzzle from the bits and pieces I was given but there was so much that didn't add up. I was frustrated because she had just began to see me as just a little sister and not an annoying brat. We were building our sisterhood and it was so cool. She was the closest sibling to me and she was 6 years my senior. She was such an amazing person who touched so many lives. I wanted to be around her as much as I could because she was so inspiring and freaking gorgeous! When her baby daddy brought another girl to my sister's funeral, wearing my sister's coat, my whole family was ready to fight! My tears dried up quick and I was ready to throw hands.

The fighting pattern continued in high school until this one boy tried it and I introduced his face to my palm. He then tried to stand up as if he was going to hit me and my god-brother stepped in. When he moved, the entire football team followed him. I don't bother nobody but I'm also not gone let nobody bother me. I guess that display of support stopped dudes from wanting problems with me. Then there was this one girl that wanted smoke with me. Now I was never suspended for any altercations with the dudes but I sure got suspended for this trick. What's crazy is I didn't even fight her! She wanted to fight me so bad but when it came down to it she was scared. I swung on her and someone grabbed me and I missed her nose by a hair. She was so scared she didn't return school after that.

When I was in high school, I loved going to my dad's house but I LOVED being at my mom's house. That was the house I referred to as home. Being at my home I knew there would always be a new adventure instead of having to travel for adventure like I did with my dad. Once I was about 15 I wasn't taking those road trips with him like I used to. I wanted to be at home on the block in the summer. Or with my mom's side of the family having some crazy type of family fun. Honestly, I was so happy when I was outside with my friends from the block. The summer time was the best time! When one of the homies came outside and did the Tarzan call, everybody slide outside within minutes and found a porch to meet up on. When we weren't outside on the porch, we went to the center, which was a community center ran by a local church in the area. I didn't get to go much but when I went, I had fun. It was everything in there! I wasn't able to do a lot of stuff away from home. My mom was pretty strict when it came to me going with friends and stuff.

My best chance was going with friends from church on Sundays when we had afternoon service. I guess she felt like it wouldn't be too much time to really get into anything. If they weren't church friends or family, the odds of me attending or being involved was low. Thinking back on it now, I guess she was just trying to protect me since I had been violated before, once by a family member and once by a neighbor. She was so close to the incidents, yet she was so far. Although I didn't initially tell her about the neighbor, I guess she carried some guilt about the family member and didn't really know how to deal with it other than keeping me away from most people and situations. As an adult, and a parent, it makes perfect sense. However, I was a child and I hated it. I wanted to be able to have fun and go out and experience life. Then I got my chance. It just wasn't in the way I wanted it.

I remember it vividly. It was a summer night and I was outside with my homies from the block. I remember seeing her car roll down the street and pull into the driveway across the street so that she could back into ours. It was the only way she would go into the driveway. When I saw her come home, I wasn't tripping because I was still up and chilling. I knew I had to do the dishes before I went to bed and I was prepared for that. I guess she wasn't satisfied with that idea so once she walked in and saw the dishes, she walked back outside and yelled for me. I answered her and began to walk towards her as she's asking me why the dishes aren't done and why I didn't change granny. My grandmother was living with us during this time and I often helped my mom take care of her. I remembered about having to do the dishes but I forgot to change my grandmother's diaper before I went outside. My mother was so upset with me that by the time I reached the lawn of the next door neighbor, she was tackling me. I'm trying to escape her grasp and she trying to sink in her claws. In the moment, I was trying hard to refrain from fighting my mother. Even though I felt like she was attacking me. I couldn't believe this was happening to me. I felt like she was overreacting. I also felt like I couldn't stay there anymore.

My boyfriend at the time was 21, I believe I was 17. I broke free from her and ran inside to call him. I locked my door and packed up what I could in a trash bag. I don't know what my mom was doing at that point. I just was trying to make sure she didn't have another skeleton key to get into my room while I was packing. I told him what happened and he asked his parents if I could come stay with them. Once they said yes, he immediately came to get me. Just like my mom, he had a red thunderbird at the time, but his was a really bright candy apple red with the tinted windows, sound system, and all that. I stayed locked in my room until he told me he was outside. Once he was out front, I unlocked the door and ran out of my room, past my mother's room, down the stairs, and out of the front door. When I got in the car my boyfriend said I looked like I was attacked by a rapist or something. He was shook. He didn't really know what to say and I just sat there in tears and in fear.

I don't know what set my mom off that day but I knew I never wanted to go through that with her again. I stayed away for a while and our relationship remained estranged. All the while I still wanted to have a bond with her. I knew I couldn't give up on that. I also knew it was best for us to be apart while we attempt to rebuild. The separation didn't last long because my mom told me that she wouldn't do anything for me for senior year, which was about to kick off, if I was still living with my boyfriend. Since I still needed her, I went back. I didn't expect my boyfriend's parents to take over in that sense. At that time staying with my dad felt more like a punishment because I would be so far away from the majority of my friends! I figured, going back was the best option. It was hard being back there. My sister got involved before I came home and had an open discussion about how we were feeling about the situation. She kinda acted as the mediator between me and my mom.

Before I knew it, I was graduating from high school. I had my sights set on California State University in Sacramento. I was accepted and filing out my housing paperwork then my dad called. He told me that he didn't want me going all the way out there because he wouldn't be able to help me if I was in California and he's still in Detroit. He ended up convincing me that I should stay close. I was slick reminded of the decision he made to stay close to me years ago and wanted to show my appreciation by honoring his request. I was devastated. I ended up attending Oakland University in Rochester, MI instead. Oakland was only about 30 minutes from Detroit and I had already been accepted there so the transition wasn't too bad. Since it was so close, I knew a few people that were there so it kinda felt like home.

My roommate was so cool freshman year. Not only did I have a dope roommate, I had a suite mate who shared a name that I thought was unique to me. I felt like I wasn't singled out by name for once in my life. That was crazy because although we share the same first name we spelled them slightly different. In addition, out appearances were different so it was easy for people to distinguish between the two of us as we got to know people on campus. My roommate and I eventually started doing hair on campus to make some money. We had a great time meeting people from various walks of life and being introduced first hand to the organizations and sororities on campus. We had so much fun living in the dorms. My roommate and I got along so well that we chose to stay together again sophomore year.

By then I had broken up with the boyfriend that I had for the previous four years. He had cheated on me and gave me an STD. Even ended up staying with him and his mom for the summer after freshman year and there was one young lady that just kept calling the house phone looking for my boyfriend. I watched the phone ring and ring the first few times cause I thought it must have been a mistake. My intuition must have kicked in because something told me to answer the next time this number popped up on the caller ID. I mean, it was Burger King showing up on the screen so I was really thinking it was an accident at first. When I answered I learned the truth. The young lady on the other end was calling to speak to my man. I politely told her he was unavailable and took a message like I was his cousin or sister or somebody cause I wanted to know what she was gonna say and how he was gonna explain himself.

Of course he was more upset with me for answering the phone than he was remorseful for cheating. So I figured it was best to go ahead and cut ties. During sophomore year I started working in the OC which was like the student union as a manager for the information desk. I was so proud of myself for getting that job because it came with a lot of responsibility and I liked that. After breaking up with my ex he started calling my roommate trying to get her to convince me to talk back to him or at least hear him out. He was so sorry and so sad that he lost me. One day, while I was working at the information desk, he came to see me. He asked me to talk to him and I agreed. I came from behind the desk and went to a little side area to talk. Within seconds he was down on one knee proposing marriage and confessing his love.

I can't lie, I was shook! I had no idea this was

coming and I was completely caught off guard. Being that I felt like I was in love with him, I said yes. I began making wedding plans and everything. I was so excited. Month after month his attention seemed to be somewhere else. I didn't seem to really be a priority for him. I stayed a little longer and learned that the ring he gave me was a fake ring that someone else purchased to give to another woman. Dude didn't even have the decency to go get a ring for me himself. That, along with his constant disinterest in planning a wedding, showed me that it was time to say goodbye once and for all. So after about 6 months of being engaged, I was single again. So I did what most young women my age was doing at the time and went to the strip club!

That was our place of release in some moments. The drinks were good and the men were nice to look at. Oh yeah, we had two male strip clubs in Detroit but one was my favorite. I frequented the spot and ended up catching the eye of a few of the dancers. One of them began to show serious interest and we started trying to get to know each other. Things were going well and he even came to visit me at school one time. I was so into him and he seemed to be so into me. We were really vibing and things were going well. Then there was a knock at my window. My ex was at the school demanding that I give him back anything he ever gave me. I was confused to say the least. I was also very pissed because I had company and my ex was there acting out.

The new guy was not feeling the stalker vibes from my ex and went to take refuge across the hall with my roommates. At this point, we were living in the first set of campus apartments. My ex had been to the apartments and was familiar with the layout and the entrance restrictions. He knew he couldn't get in without someone granting him access. The new guy didn't know that nor did he feel safe or comfortable with the situation. It really got stressful because my ex was beating on the window and demanding access to the apartment. At some point he convinced someone to let him in the front entrance and then he was able to come and knock on the apartment door. My roommates were unsure of what to do so I locked myself in my room and told them not to let me in. We were all scared at this point. My ex was 6'5" and over 250 pounds. We were 4 girls and 1 guy deep and none of us really wanted to deal with this.

He eventually left after I called campus police and the banned him from ever coming to campus again. The new guy felt so unsafe and unsettled, he decided not to continue getting to know me. Once I took him home, we didn't speak more than sharing cordial greetings in passing. I was kinda hurt because I felt like he let the actions of my ex completely change his feelings about me. It made me feel a little like he didn't really like me that much from the beginning. I didn't stay sad long though. There were so many things going on around campus to keep me occupied and busy. One of my favorite things to do was go to the campus parties. The sororities and fraternities always threw the best parties! At one of the parties I met this guy who was fine as hell! He was a little short but he was fine and I was interested.

We began getting to know each other as friends after he asked me to braid his hair. He became one of my regular clients and one of my closest male friends there. The crazy part was he wasn't even a student, his brother was. I knew his brother first because he was the one all the upper class girls warned us about when we first got to campus. I kept my guard up around him and we actually became pretty cool. When I met his brother I was like, damn! He was just as fine and he seemed really sweet and genuine. After a few months of braiding his hair and talking to him about other dudes I was talking to, he ended up telling me that he was interested in taking our friendship to another level. I was so intrigued by him so I decided to give him a chance and see what he was trying to do.

Things were cool with us for awhile. It was a crazy ride and I was down for it. Then things changed for me after getting some startling news. My parents told me that they were not going to pay for the previous set of classes because it was a spring/summer quarter and they were only paying for fall and winter. I tried to get loans to pay the balance for my spring and summer quarters and I could not get the money together. I was devastated. I had to leave school and leave him. I was hurt that they weren't going to pay for that and it would cause me to have to leave. For a while I held that against them. I later released that because they were doing what they felt was best and I can respect that even if I disagree.

After leaving school he and I stayed in touch and remained in a relationship despite our distance, which was about 15 minutes. We both were without cars at this time so it was hard to see each other without the help of other people. One day, I found out that I was pregnant. Once I told him, he decided to join the military. That was the best option for us. Once he joined I ended up moving back in with my mother to get as much help as I could until it was time to go be with him. He asked me where I wanted to live and I told him all southern states. So after he finished all of his training he ended up getting orders to Georgia. I was happy because I really wanted to be down south. He lived down there without me for a few months. When I was roughly 8 months pregnant he came home and we got married. It was a really small wedding with just my mom, my sister, my niece, and the two witnesses (who were our friends from Oakland).

When my dad found out I was pregnant, he ended up buying me a little cash car. I was so happy to have a car again. I was able to pick my man up and drive us to the church to get married. After the wedding, he took the car and went to go see his family. Yet he didn't tell them we were married until months later. He actually got upset with me because my younger cousin was attending Oakland with his older brother and the news spread in my family. So she ended up saying something to his brother and he was pissed! He felt like I had no right to share his business, even though it was my business too. Anywho, I was due a month after we got married and due to some medical concerns the doctors ended up inducing my labor about a week early. When the baby was born she was amazing! She didn't have any of the medical concerns they mentioned. She did have to be tested to confirm that she had Down syndrome.

The doctors had already told me about that when I was about 4-5 months pregnant after my quad test. I immediately told my man about it and he calmed me down and told me it would be okay. When I got the news I was sitting alone in a white room at the hospital. I was terrified, so his words of comfort really helped. Once our daughter was two weeks old we were cleared to travel and move to our new home on the military base in Georgia. My dad offered to drive me and the baby down for out last road trip together as he handed me off to my husband. My dad packed up his truck with my initials on the doors and drove us 12 hours to Georgia. Once he unloaded the truck and got us settled in, he turned around and got right back on the road to head home. I appreciated him so much for that. It meant a lot to me.

After my dad left, my husband went to work. Me and the baby were left there alone. Things continued to go up and down in the marriage over the course of 7 years. We ended up having three kids together and despite building a family, we decided to part ways after those 7 years. By the time we were divorced, we were 8 years in. It was a rough adjustment for us. I ended up completing my bachelors degree during the marriage and started my masters. Things ended up getting really crazy and I made the choice to stop school and go back to work. I was so close to completing my masters in mental health but I was at the point where I had to do unpaid training and I was a new single parent who had to provide for my kids.

I started selling cars and I was making decent money. Things were improving for us. I was able to move us from an apartment into a house and I was really proud of that. Things got weird at work after my ex-husband's new wife came to the car dealership attempting to stir the pot and cause problems. I ended up moving to another city in Georgia where the company had another dealership. I was placed in a new position and my pay was slightly increased. I was told it was a lateral move and I was given more responsibility. It was cool until it wasn't. I was forced to work on Saturday and since I didn't have a sitter, I told them I had to bring my kids with me. Since I had my own office, they agreed. My kids have been with me through thick and thin and have always been down for whatever. As long as they were with me, we were alright. That job started getting weird and I had to think about making a move to a new job. I bounced around to a few different dealerships until I got out of the car business. It was an extremely difficult terrain to navigate because my dad died during all of this as well. I was crushed. My dad was the one person that I felt really cared about me and would bite the claws off a bear for me. Seeing my parent in a casket was something I knew I could never do again.

Later on, I ended up working for the state as a temp and actually got hired on in another department. I liked the job until the head man in charge started moving funny. I'm not one to let people talk to me any kinda way so if they try, I set them straight regardless of who they are or the title they held. I was working there and still living below the poverty line. To me, that didn't make sense! When this was mentioned to the head man, he offered to give me more money if I accepted more responsibilities. I declined and ended up moving back to where I lived when I sold cars. While I was working for the state, I published my first book and started my publishing company when I moved back to the city I used to live in. I went back to the dealership I was at before since I had such a good rapport with everyone there, it was a smooth transition.

This time when I came back, they wanted me to work in another department and I killed it! Eventually I asked to be over the department because I was more productive, more respected, and more involved than the manager they currently had. The two things he had over me were balls and white skin. Those two things kept me from getting that position. They strung me along for awhile. Until it all got turned around on me. The general manager decided to have a contest for those of us in my department. Our job was to call customers or work incoming calls and get customers to schedule appointments to speak with a sales rep. We were given a daily, weekly, and monthly goal. For this contest, I knew it would be easy to win. That's exactly what I did! I bodied this contest!!! I ended up winning a weekend off, $100 spending cash, and a 2 night stay at the Hyatt.

When I took my little getaway, things fell apart at work and new rules were implemented as a result of everyone else's performance. When I returned they wanted me to fall in line with the new rules but I only learned about them when I was doing something and was corrected. No one came and told me about all of the changes until I made a mistake. I got irritated quickly behind being kept in the dark but being expected to excel. My manager, the one who's job I wanted, ended up telling me everything. I explained to him that it is not fair for me to have to abide by these new rules as they were put in place as punishment for something that was done while I was away. He tried to swing his balls and I called his bluff. They ended up terminating me and saying that I quit. I appealed the case with unemployment and won. I knew I wouldn't be able to go back there anymore for work.

Since I had such great relationships there, I was able to go back periodically and sell my books and even sell plates of food with the help of one of my favorite coworkers! He was basically like my very own street team. Anything I was involved in, he was supporting!

It felt so good to be able to live a piece of my dream. I was, and still am, very grateful to all who supported me! My friend was so down for me that even when he left the dealership that we worked at together, he promoted whatever I had to everyone at his new job. He helped me so much and I will always appreciate him for that! By this time, I published my second book and my publishing company was starting to pick up some buzz. My skills as a writer placed me in a number of situations. Some were amazing, while some were traps. I had to learn quickly that some people will recognize your gifts and try to use them up for their benefit while you are left drained.

    I knew all too well what being drained felt like. I was pulled in every direction possible during this time. I was trying to develop a successful business and still fighting battles with my ex-husband, even though we weren't even speaking outside of court due to the permanent restraining order. I was living in a townhouse that was not kept up to parr and fighting with the landlord about that. I was dealing with the stressors of single parenting while trying not to lose my mind. It was a rough time in life for me. I often felt alone and beat down. I felt like I was making all the wrong moves and poor decisions. I was extremely hard on myself and I just wanted to provide for my kids. I saw how unfair the workforce was and I knew that I didn't want to go back. I saw how horrible my ex-husband was to us and I knew I could only depend on him to continue being him. I can't lie, my marriage really took a toll on me. I endured a lot within those seven years and I felt like damaged goods for the first 4-5 years after the divorce.

I did my best to keep my kids as stable as possible. Once I left the city again, I went to an Atlanta suburb and we lived there for a couple of years. I searched and searched and searched for jobs until I finally got something through a temp agency. The shift I was working was 2-10 and that was hard on me because I wasn't really seeing my kids and they had to be home alone all that time. When the chance came to move to a better shift, that's what I did. Apparently the area that I moved to, was very comfortable with the workers they had and didn't really want new people coming in. It was very much like high school. The popular kids said what was going to happen and that's what happened. I had a couple friends there and we were all targeted as the ones who had to go.

One day while we were working, my friends and I decided that we were going to take our break together once another group came back from theirs. I guess this was a prime time for the plot to thicken because that's exactly what it did. While we were on break, someone closed the door that gave us access to the break room and locked us out. They didn't lock just us out though, but they did cause us to be late returning from break. As soon as we returned, we were pulled aside and told to leave because we were terminated. I couldn't believe what I was being told. I thought she was joking at first, because she wanted to be a cool manager and played around sometimes. This time, she was serious, but we were set up! Needless to say, I was pissed!

One of the girls that got fired with me was actually a friend of mine and we decided to start a business together. She was the graphic designer and I was the writer. We developed a business that helped small businesses brand themselves. We were the first ones to put QR codes on our clothes to market ourselves. We had an office space and things seemed to be going fairly well. The one thing that slowed us down was consistency. Our personal struggles made it hard for us to be as consistent as we wanted to be. We started out doing crafts and it quickly shifted to more business consulting with customized business items. We became promotional product distributors and we were feeling it. Our colors stood out and so did we! Despite our buzz, our finances were low. Just as fast as it was taking off, it started to dwindle at that same rate. People saw what we had to offer and would 'pick our brain' for information and pick our pockets for money. The more we had meetings with people who just wanted to know what we could do for them, the more we realized this was something we needed to charge for. They already weren't paying us without us charging so when we started charging for consults, business dropped. Our personal lives then began to overshadow the business and we had to let the building go.

As the front face and voice of the business, I took

a lot of responsibility for our success and our demise. I felt like I couldn't do nothing right. I felt like I was drowning under the pressure. I felt like I wouldn't be able to properly take care of my kids. I ended up getting into an accident and things just continued to spiral from there. It got to the point where I ended up calling my brothers on my dad's side for help. I simply told my brothers that I was on the verge of a nervous breakdown and I needed help. I couldn't keep going on the way that I was. One of my brothers offered for my kids and I to move to Tennessee with him. He said we could stay there as long as we needed to and he would take care of everything. I was so grateful to have this opportunity but I was also saddened by the fact that I would have to leave the place I've called home for the previous 14 years. I had made so many genuine connections during that time, I was really saddened to have to leave because I knew the dynamics of the relationships would change. At the same time, I needed the help.

In February 2019, my three kids and our little chiweenie packed up and moved to Tennessee with one of my brothers. It took me a few months to find a job but I was happy that I was able to breathe again. It felt like I was going to be able to get my feet back on solid ground. I was and still am, very grateful to my brother for letting us live there. He had two spare rooms and a full shed for us to utilize. My girls shared a bed in one room and my son had the other room. I would take a couch or sleep in the shed. The shed was big enough to be a studio apartment and it had heating and air hooked up. It was set up nicely. The only thing it didn't have was plumbing so there was no bathroom or kitchen to use over there. I didn't mind walking back into the house for that. I was so happy to be able to be with family and have support, I really didn't care about much else. Then I met this dude on a dating app. He seemed like he was a good dude who had just fallen on hard times. Me being me, I felt like I could help him because he appeared to be already helping himself. Little did I know, this was something he did regularly. He would meet women, get to know them, and take advantage of them however he could.

By the time I realized his game plan, he was living in the shed and I was living back in the house. Things were starting to get weird with him because he realized that he didn't have me on the hook anymore. We were both working at the same place but October 2019. I was moving up at the job and he was moving on. He started talking to someone else and things were getting messy. He was still living with us and was paying off a car he purchased from my brother. He had all of his possessions in the shed. I told him that he needed to get his things and complete his transition but he said he didn't have to since it was my brothers home and he would get everything straight with him. I left it alone and continued to climb the ladder at work. By December, this guy was gone from work, the shed, and my life. I was done giving chances to men and I was only entertaining what benefited me.

While at work one day, I was approached by a coworker who was giving me game on the job and how I could climb up. He was the reason I was moving the way I was at the job. Once things ended with the other dude, I ended up giving the new dude a shot. I didn't want anything more than a physical relationship and he was down with that so that's where it all started. He and I grew closer and closer as friends during this process, even though that was the opposite of what we wanted when we started this. Yet and still, it was nice. After the first year of our interaction, it was still very clear that we were just friends who liked being around each other and it wouldn't really go past there. Then years continued to pass and we were still in each other's lives. We were more invested than ever before. Our children were involved. We were taking family trips. We even looked at places to rent together.

He came and showed me something that I didn't even know I needed to see. I later learned that I did the same thing for him. Our bond continued to grow no matter how hard we tried to fight it. We became so connected that it seemed like we were inseparable. Years continued to move and our dynamic started to shift. We began building things together. He gave me money to invest in stocks, we decided to share a bank account, and even swapped keys when we each purchased our own homes. He has really been my rock and my soft place. I feel like he is my reward after all the crap I've been through.

I can honestly say that moving to Tennessee was

the best thing I could have done for my family. I restarted my writing and publishing company, Creative Chameleon and things began to happen. I made new connections at work who helped sell books and merchandise. I met my current photographer there as well. I had great insurance and I was able to provide for my kids. I hated some of the day to day crap that happened at work but I really loved my job. I felt like it would be my last job because I would retire from there. That was not the case though. Things started to shift all of a sudden and when I would call it out I was told that it was just my imagination. Then in December 2020, I got a phone call while I was sitting at my desk at work that would change my life. It was the third call within 2 minutes. I answered with the intent of letting them know that I was working and I would call them back. I never got those words out though. The caller on the other end was calling to tell me that my mom had passed.

I wish I could forget the day but it lives rent free in my mind. When my dad passed, I was prepared. I was able to see him and tell him goodbye. I was able to hold him one last time. I was able to be there with him and enjoy our last moments together. That wasn't the case with my mom. It was sudden. Once I heard the news I could do nothing but scream. I cried and tried to talk but I couldn't breathe. All of the people in the office were trying to figure out what was going on and after barely catching my breath I was able to tell them my mom was gone. I was escorted to an empty area outside of the office to collect myself. I was crushed. My mom had called me a few years prior and apologized for everything and we became really REALLY close. So to hear that she was no longer here broke me. I had finally gotten a chance to have what I fought so hard for. I finally knew what it was like for my mom to be there for me and really be my friend. I finally knew what it was like to want to talk to her instead of talking to her out of necessity. I was so grateful for her apology that I immediately accepted it and we just became the best of friends. As I prepared to travel back to Detroit to assist my remaining siblings with the funeral plans, I had to maintain my composure because I didn't have the guts to tell my kids alone.

My mom had become my biggest supporter. My kids loved their Nana. I waited till we reached Detroit and went to my sister's house. We told them together and I was happy that there was someone there for each of us. It was the hardest thing I have ever had to do in my life. With my dad, my siblings handled everything because they are all more than 15 years older than me and I had young kids. I wasn't in any position to be of assistance. With my mom, it was different. My kids were teenagers, I was working a good job, and there were only 3 of us left to do it. My sister and I found so much stuff when we started cleaning out the house. I ended up going back and forth between Detroit and Tennessee for about 4 months after the funeral. I went back to work in January so I would use my off days, once a month and drive up to help my sister clean up the house. I learned so much about my mom while we sifted through her things. This process was hard but it gave me a lot of peace because I knew she had obtained the peace she needed before she left here.

Things were moving along with the house but work was moving in a different direction. While I was away, one of the guys in the office took over my responsibilities. When I came back, it was hard for him to give those duties back to me. Before too long, things were getting really weird and I was being pulled out of the office for unwarranted reasons. Honestly, I was being targeted. I asked what the next steps were for me because I could sense the shift in the energy of the room and I could tell they wanted me gone. Again, I am not one to bite my tongue, so when I see something, I say something. When I said something prior to my mom's passing, it was all good but once I came back from that it was like I wasn't allowed to speak or even do my job. Nevertheless, I kept showing up and kept being great. All of a sudden I was removed from my office job and placed back on the floor in the warehouse. It was the middle of May and the temperatures were already climbing so it was just a matter of time before things would get rough for me.

My asthma began to be aggravated by the elevated temps in the warehouse and it was extremely difficult to breathe. I kept showing up and kept going through the motions until one day my body had a serious reaction to the heat. I walked in just like the days before. I had a decent meal before work, I filled up my water bottle and used the restroom, I went to my area to setup for the day. All of a sudden I started to feel heat rising from my feet like I was burning from the inside out. My coworker asked me if I was ok and I shook my head 'no' because I knew something was off. I don't remember much about all of the steps that followed but I do recall being walked into a cool room and having ice placed on me. I remember them asking me questions and my hands being stiff and stuck. I remember not feeling the ice when they put it on me and I remember trying to tell them I have asthma. Then I remember shivering and shaking uncontrollably. One of the ladies that was in there helping me was a nurse and she said that I was headed into a heat stroke from severe heat exhaustion. I was terrified. Once I was cool and coherent enough, they let me drive home.

That was the beginning of the end for me at the job. When I came back it was a non stop battle trying to get me moved somewhere else so that I could do my job without being subjected to possible heat related issues. I soon learned that the goal was to get me to quit, not for them to help. I fought as long and as hard as I could until I ended up on antidepressants with a psychiatrist and seeing a therapist regularly. I was made to feel like I was the wrong one and when I was right, I was too slow to have anything done about it. Time just wasn't on my side. When I got the information, it didn't apply to my situation. It was always something. Some sort of red tape or crazy hoops to jump through. After over a year and a half of fighting, I gave up and I quit. I quit taking the anti-depressants, I quit the company, I quit therapy, I quit it all.

I refocused my energy and dove back into writing and poetry. I started performing and reading my poems live on stages any chance I got. I performed for large audiences at major venues and I've performed on small stages at hole in the walls. I have made a name for myself in my local poetry community. I have been interviewed for magazines, blogs, and even slid onto a major radio platform. I have published more books for myself and clients! My business has picked up and things have begun to move in an upward direction. To say that I am grateful would be a vast understatement. I have done so many things and helped so many people learn how to love themselves and be truthful with themselves. I have impacted lives through my events and my books. I know that I went through all of what I went through because I need to be a pillar for someone else. I always knew I wasn't just living for me. I didn't survive all of these tests and trials to sit back and watch other people struggle through.

I was made for greatness! I was made to inspire and to make a difference. I was made to help. I am proud to say that in 2024 two of my children are high school graduates and my baby will graduate in 2025. Despite the road, we made it to our destination. These three little people have been my riders for awhile. It is bittersweet to see them transition into this new stage of life but it is very exciting nonetheless. I hurt sometimes because my parents aren't physically here to see them move on to the next level. At the same time, I am happy that they did get to meet them and share some moments with them. I know my parents are smiling as they watch from the distance. I know that I have even more things to accomplish and to achieve. I know that my journey is not over, it's just beginning. I appreciate everyone that believed in my vision and said yes anytime I asked.

Tiffany, Renato, Shannon, and Naya, THANK YOU! You believed in this vision and agreed to be apart of it. I know that one of my callings is to give a voice to the voiceless and you ladies helped me to do that. Our stories will shed light on what so many try to hide in the dark. Our stories will start conversations that so many were afraid to have. Our stories will be a catalyst for healing for so many who thought they could never be fixed. This book is not the end. This book is just an introduction. I wanted the world to see that Detroit produces greatness. Despite the hardships and rough times, Detroit taught us all grit and grind. Detroit made us who we are and I know we wouldn't have it any other way! So when people inquire about our greatness, we can all sit back and say with pride, it started off with 'Just A Girl From Detroit'!

Shay Cole

Born and raised in Detroit, MI, Shay Cole has been a writer and an entrepreneur for most of her life. She started out writing in middles school. She wrote a lot of poetry and short stories as a young lady and even won a few poetry competitions. She began her entrepreneurial journey in direct sales. Her first product was candles. While figuring out if she wanted to stick with being an entrepreneur or move into the corporate workforce, she attended Oakland University and studied Psychology. During her time at Oakland she made a name for herself with her poetry and writing abilities. After her first 3 years, she took some time off to start a family.

Shay went back to school after her third child was born to complete her first degree. During her early years of child rearing, Shay dipped her hands back into direct sales and even started a few businesses of her own. She had a company creating custom business stationary for local military members and ran a successful home daycare.

In 2014, Shay published her first book and started Creative Chameleon in 2015. She wanted to help others tell their stories and provide a platform for them to do so.

In 2019, Shay began to dabble in promotional product sales and really enjoyed it. Shay had so much fun helping others with business branding through promotional products she added the services to Creative Chameleon.

Shay began to perform her poetry regularly in 2022. She got her feet wet performing at the City Winery in Nashville. The following year, Shay decided to add travel advisor to her skillset in 2023. After 10 years of planning, Shay Cole has started her non-profit, The P.E.A.C.E. Movement which is geared towards helping domestic violence survivors, poverty stricken individuals, and those transitioning from military to civilian life.

Renato L. Friday

Renato was born and raised in Detroit, Michigan. She's always had a love of reading and writing, but never thought about becoming an author. She started writing poetry at the age of 15 and continued throughout adulthood. After things started changing in her life, she turned to writing as her therapy and wanted to tell the world her story, which was the birth of her memoir: Through the Rain. To date, she has written a poetry book, a novel, a short story, a children's book and 3 novellas, and this Detroit girl shows no sign of slowing down any time soon.

Naya Perry-Eddings

Naya Perry-Eddings was born and raised on the westside of Detroit with her mother and older brother. She is a proud Navy veteran who is making a huge impact in a small city. Naya is affectionately known as "DJ Royalty" to her clients and local community. She creates the vibe with music and personality at a variety of events.

Naya is also an amazing wife, mother, and friend to so many. Her generosity has been a huge part of her impact in her community. She uplifts, encourages, and motivates everyone she encounters. Naya was involved in her first writing project by participating in the book, "From His Partner to His Prey". Naya now officially adds author to her list of accomplishments. She is always setting goals and achieving them with style and grace. Naya is "Just A Girl From Detroit" who you need to know.

Tiffany Barber

Tiffany "T.Barb" Barber is a comedian and actress who quit a 14 year social work career to pursue her dreams. As a first generation college graduate Tiffany broke the curse of incarceration in her family, never allowing the odds to beat her. Born and raised in Detroit, she attended HBCU Dillard University and later received her MBA from The University of Detroit Mercy, beating all the odds placed against her. Always known for being funny and keeping a smile, she discovered stand up comedy & has been blazing stages since! Known for her hardworking nature, comedic versatility, sharp improv, unique style & likable personality, she is the perfect fit for any project. T.Barb's favorite quote is "You Don't Have To Stay Where You Start", because she never allowed humble beginnings to dictate her destiny.

In addition to being a comedian and actress, T.Barb is also an author, vegan chef, philanthropist, producer, mother and motivational speaker. She has a passion for people and the community and uses her celebrity to benefit a multitude of organizations including her own non profit, T.Barb and Friends.

Shannon Cain-Womack

My name is Shannon Cain-Womack I was born in Detroit, Michigan raised by my two amazing parents. Attending Detroit Public Schools Elementary, St. Raymond's Catholic School and graduating from Jared W. Finney with my high school diploma in June of 2000. From there she went to Oakland University, home of the "Grizzlies". Majoring in Communication with a minor in Marketing. I'm the proud mother of two beautiful, smart and talented young ladies. And a proud first time grandmother of an adorable baby boy as of 2023.

As a young girl I began designing and sketching clothes later on in the years I developed a love for modeling and wanted to be a model someday many and here I'm today a true fashionista. I've been writing since I was a young girl. I found joy in writing short stories and would later win a writing competition getting a signed President's Award along with many other writing awards. Growing up I used to write songs in hopes that Brandy, Monica or Whitney Houston (her auntie in her head) would sing. I would babysit my cousins to keep them occupied. I would teach them songs word for word and make up their choreography. They probably wanted to call me cousin "Joe".

I began working in the caregiving field in 2009 caring for people in adult foster care and the elderly in nursing homes. I Currently work in Utilization Management managing prior authorizations for durable medical equipment. I'm known to be a caring person with a big heart. My family and friends would describe me as being funny, bubbly and full of life. I love traveling and creating new memories with the people I love.

I have some enthralling life's stories, some good, some bad and a nightmare that would change my life forever. Nevertheless, these situations are what shaped me into the woman that I am today and the woman I'm going to become in the future. No matter where I am or how far I'm going I'm forever going to be "JUST A GIRL FROM DETROIT".

www.ingramcontent.com/pod-product-compliance
Lightning Source LLC
Chambersburg PA
CBHW072211070526
44585CB00015B/1290